MADE FROM SCRATCH

A Recipe for Success

Nella Curatolo

MADE FROM SCRATCH

Nella Curatolo

Published By:
Puget Sound Press
6523 California Ave., S.W.
PMB 292
Seattle, WA 98136-1833
http://www. pugetsoundpress.com
email: thezo@sprintmail.com

ISBN: 0-9660092-3-1
Library of Congress Catalog Number: 99-60375

Cover design by: Christina A. Webb
Photographs of Italy by: Dianne Kraus
Photographs of Gioacchino's by: Marta and Louis Nealy
All photographs are the property of Nella Curatolo

Printed in the United States of America

1 2 3 4 5 6 7 8 9

MADE FROM SCRATCH

Puget Sound Press   Seattle

DEDICATION

I dedicate this book to both my mother and my father. There is no greater love than the love that I carry in my heart for them. My mother passed away before she could experience the rewards in raising a daughter to respect and love her family.

I honor my mother for teaching me the meaning of sharing with others in order to have more. I honor my father for validating me as a woman with good decision- making abilities and the ability to remain committed to my dreams. I thank you both for your love and support.

Nella Curatolo

CONTENTS

Front Row: Right to left
Emilia Nella Mother Maria Orlando

Front Row: Left to Right
Nella Mother Maria
Back Row: Left to Right
Mario Rocco

Nella's
Mother

Nella is second from the right

Pictures of Italy

Nella

Nella   **Bianca**   **Jack**

INTRODUCTION

It is an honor to have been chosen to introduce you to Nella Curatolo's first book. On the other hand, I must say in a most unpretentious way that I am the perfect person for the job: I can write, but I cannot cook. While I am embarrassed to admit that I am an Italian-American woman on the brink of the twenty-first century who cannot do both, I am proud to have the opportunity to publicly thank Nella Curatolo for sustaining me over the years with her wonderful foods and for providing me many times with "food for thought as well."

Over the years, I have dedicated a large portion of my life to knowing about, reading about, and writing about Italian-Americans who personify history-changing, noteworthy attributes of our heritage. From the genius of Dante Alighieri, Michelangelo, and DaVinci; the courage of Vespucci; the perseverance of Columbus; untouchable sports legacies like DiMaggio; entertainment giants like Sinatra; and leaders in science, art, politics, religion, and fashion—Italian-Americans have either paved the way, changed the way, or did it "their way" with unsurpassed results and charisma.

Enter Nella Curatolo, a woman who most definitely exemplifies a full array of the uniquely Italian attributes. To know her as I have is to see much more than a successful businesswoman, an extremely well known individual, and an outstanding cook. Beyond her beaming and seemingly tireless exterior is a never-ending font of hospitality, unselfishness, and unwavering loyalty to her family, a commitment to community that is more action than words, and a friend that is unable to say "no" in either Italian or English.

Not only am I unable to cook a simple pot of pastina, but I have not yet traveled to Italy, home of my ancestors–home to a heritage of food with heart and soul to which no other country in the universe can compare. Nella Curatolo is my trip to Italy personified: a breath of fresh seaside air, groves of the finest olives as far as the eye can see, and the excitement of people who speak the world's most romantic language and yet talk with their hands as well. Nella Curatolo takes us all into her mother's kitchen with each meal that she abundantly prepares.

Nella dedicates this book to her mother, a woman I have never met, but one that I can vividly imagine standing at a humble stove in a modest "cucina," setting the table for her nine children, saturating the surroundings with the fragrances of fresh herbs, homemade pasta, and fresh vegetables. I can picture Nella absorbing it all like a human sponge. And so, I take this moment to thoughtfully thank Mrs. Ruffolo for giving us Nella and for somehow instilling in her a passion not for cooking alone, but for life. Mrs. Ruffolo would burst with pride to see Nella today: accomplished yet rooted in strong values and a mother herself to her beautiful daughter Bianca.

In a world of fast food, heartburn (or "agita," as we Italians call it), and families that no longer come together at the dinner table, Nella and her restaurants are a veritable oasis. They are the next best thing to being home; and Nella is the next best thing to having our own mothers cook for us. It doesn't get any better.

I have watched the renowned Italian cook/restaurateur Biba Caggiano on television many times, silently applauding her for her "uncomplicated, straightforward" way of cooking. Biba and Nella have much in common.

3

In one of Biba's books, she writes, "Without Italy, this book would not be possible." Nella, no doubt, shares these sentiments. Furthermore, I am confident that one day I will turn on my television and find Nella on the airwaves making mouths water, too.

I am sure that Nella is grateful to those who were there for her through the days of painful persecution and deeply hurt feelings and the days of negativity from those who were convinced that Nella, a woman and an immigrant, stood no chance of living the American Dream. No one handed Nella Curatolo success on a silver platter. She did it on her own, making her story that much more admirable. How will bookstores file this book on the shelves? More than a cookbook, more than an autobiography, more than a how-to, it is more like a volume of motivation; bottled energy in book form.

I am proud to present my friend, Nella Curatolo, and her story. It is an account of a life that can only inspire others to work toward the fulfillment of their goals and dreams, to keep at it when they are weary and discouraged, to push when they are too tired to stand up, to do it especially when others say it can't be done. To Nella and those who follow in her footsteps, I say, "Salud!"

I am a huge fan of the late teacher/motivator, Leo Buscaglia. He wrote often of his trials as the son of

Italian immigrants. He also writes of the memories no one can take from him: of fun, of fun, and of operas. His words remind me of Nella: "Life is not a trip in itself. It's not a goal. It's a process. You get there step by step by step by step....Choose the way of love. Choose the way of caring. Choose the way of hope. Choose the way of goodness." He did. So has Nella.

As I said of Nella in a piece recently written for my own magazine, Nella and her husband Jack never rest on their laurels. They are as hard working as ever and believe strongly in giving to others without expecting to get anything back in return. Her generosity and kindness precede her wherever she goes, and it is these qualities, among many others, that make Nella Curatolo the boss in her kitchen, a friend among friends, and "the salt of the earth."

Tina Valentino
Editor/Publisher of the *Melrose Parker*
magazine and other publications

"Nella is one of those individuals who always, always does the right thing. People like that are an inspiration to those around them. It should come as no surprise, then, that everyone who knows Nella is a better person for it."

Paul Basile, Editor, *Fra Noi*, Chicagoland's Italian-American Voice

CHAPTER 1

The Old Country:
The Dream Is Born

Historically speaking, Italians have been known for their storytelling. I would like to share with you a story that was told to my husband, Jack, and myself by a food supplier to our restaurants, who also happens to be Italian. This special story is about a hard working Italian farmer named Piero. Piero's family was poor financially, but rich in tradition and love for country and family. Piero often dreamed of having expensive, delicious meals and a lovely home. However, as reality would have it, he came home every day to homemade flour soup and chopped tomatoes.

Sometimes his wife, Maria, would prepare vegetables she had not sold that day in the market–some cabbage, a few potatoes, beans, and peppers. However, more times than Piero would have liked, the family meals consisted of flour soup and chopped tomatoes. Piero and Maria worked extremely hard on their tiny farm, as did their young sons. Despite all their hard work, the family was still poor, and all they could afford was a supper of thick flour soup and chopped tomatoes.

One hot and humid day, after working extra hard on the farm, Piero was so hungry that he could hardly wait to get home to his supper. He prayed that there would be a special supper once he arrived—he longed for something different to eat. That evening, when he arrived home he single-mindedly walked straight to the pot on the wood-burning iron stove and looked in, hoping to find his prayer answered.

He didn't even speak to or look at Maria when he entered his home, hoping against hope that he would find anything but flour soup and tomatoes for supper. When he saw the thick flour soup cooking and on the table next to it a bowl of chopped tomatoes, it was just too much for him. He began shouting, and in his anger he knocked over the pot of flour soup and spilled it all over the iron top of the stove.

Maria was so upset! She, too, had worked ex-tremely hard that day and was very hungry. The sight of her thick flour soup spilled all over the stove filled her with dismay. Angrily, she picked up the bowl of chopped tomatoes and dumped them on the now-bubbling flour soup. Piero and Maria became embroiled in a terrible argument and forgot all about the spilled dinner on the hot stovetop. When they finally looked up, what they saw didn't look anything like their usual supper.

The hot plate of the stove had baked the thick soup into a flatbread with a bubbling top of chopped tomatoes. They had never seen anything like it, but they were so hungry that they ran to get a knife and each cut themselves a piece. To their surprise, it tasted wonderful. When their sons came home and smelled the toasted flatbread with bubbling tomatoes they shouted, "Dammi u pizza!" That particular dialect means, "Give me a piece!" Thus was born the first pizza!

I love this story. It reminds me so much of my own family and our humble beginnings in southern Italy, as well as the early days of living in America. Like Piero and Maria, my family originally lived on a small farm, and we were very, very poor. My family was quite large. There were nine children, and I was number eight. Originally there were fifteen children, but two different sets of twins died when approximately eight and nine months old, respectively. My mother (Teresa) also lost two babies due to miscarriages.

My earliest recollection is when I was three years old. Our farm sat in a beautiful valley. The beauty of the land was especially evident during late spring, summer, and early fall when its deep rich colors provided a gentle radiance. Once a year, usually in late May or early June, the wealthy citizens of the province would gather in the valley for a festive weekend, which included skeet shooting, bicycle races, and a farm fair with free food. It was a time to mingle with neighbors and friends for laughter and fun.

Also located in this beautiful valley about ten minutes from our plantation was a magnificent waterfall. Even though the water was very cold, my brothers still managed to learn how to swim in its basin. Some of the best tasting walnuts in the region could be located on our neighbor's farmland, which was roughly a fifteen-minute walk from our plantation. Another twenty-minute walk away sat some of the finest fig, olive, and pear trees on my grandfather's land.

I also remember how rigorous our daily lives were with respect to tending the farm. Hard work was no stranger to our family, especially during harvest time. We grew just about every vegetable there is: riapini, zucchini, cucumber, cabbage, broccoli, squash, eggplant, peppers, onion, garlic, mushrooms, carrots, cauliflower, romaine and butterhead lettuce, spinach, beets, turnips, mustard, and collard greens; you name it, we grew it.

I can recall how huge our vegetables would grow, especially our tomatoes and potatoes, which usually required hiring additional help to harvest. One such person who was always there to help our family was my mother's youngest sister, Aunt Saletta. Come to think of it, she was always present to help my mother with planting the vegetable seed, and she would be there in the fields to help us with the harvest. Aunt Saletta was one of my favorite relatives; she had an endearing and accommodating disposition. Both before and after harvest time, I couldn't help but notice my mother's gratitude for her sister's help by the affection she displayed toward Aunt Saletta.

Literally everything our family ate, sold, and made came from the land, just as it was for Piero and Maria. My mother was an excellent cook, and she taught me to cook at an early age. I was already making ravioli by the time I was eleven or twelve years old. I am proud of myself that as a little girl, cooking came naturally to me. When I was thirteen years old and living in America, I often cooked for my nieces and nephews, which in addition to my immediate family usually totaled between twenty to thirty people.

Every meal that I prepared was created from scratch with only the freshest ingredients. The first recipe that brought me immediate success was not actually a

11

traditional recipe, but rather a philosophy. Since cooking came naturally, it made perfect sense to me that in order to improve my skills I would need to follow my mother's example, which is to make each meal *from scratch*.

As I stated earlier, my childhood in Cosenza Rende, Italy was rigorous. Due to the laborious responsibilities that come with tending a farm, we had to be physically strong and emotionally dedicated to a work ethic that was second to none. I can remember my father (Umile, however, in America he was referred to as Emilio) harvesting thirty to forty acres of farmland. For fifteen years, my father took very good care of this farmland, and he looked forward to one day owning this land. He had worked extremely hard to harvest beautiful and delicious vegetables.

My father and the owner of this land had previously reached an agreement that after a designated period of time, he could purchase this farmland for an agreed upon sum of money. My father farmed this land with great anticipation of this dream becoming a reality, and he had one more year to wait. He also farmed one of the largest watermelon plantations in the valley, and I know he felt extremely proud of this and looked forward to owning this land as well. I remember so vividly how I would often stand along the roadside and sell watermelons to our faithful customers. One of my strongest memories as a child is when my father exchanged the wheat that we harvested for groceries. This is a powerful recollection for me because it represented one of the few times that we had a little money.

One spring afternoon as I was in the valley helping my mother pick potatoes on the farm, I noticed a number of automobiles driving toward our house. I asked my mother, "Who are those people?" She said, "Honey, those are the people that your father has borrowed money from. Those are called creditors. Your father owes debts." When I asked why, my mother said, "Well, because we borrow the money year-round, and now they're coming to collect, and your dad doesn't have the money. They have to come back." I was so sad when my mother told me that we didn't have the money. I realized at that point, at three years of age, that when I grew up I would never be poor. I was willing to do whatever it took to never be poor again.

Another powerful memory for me is when I accompanied my mother to Saint Rocco, a church that was one block from our house, to pray the rosary. I remember her as a peaceful and humble soul walking home after leaving the church. I did not have the words then to describe my experience with her, but as I reflect back on these experiences, this is how I would describe her today. This is what I drew from my mother: her strong sense of humility and devotion.

My mother was also an extremely hard working woman and a go-getter. I inherited my aggressiveness as well as my sense of humility from her. Her children always came first, and she was determined to make life easier for us no matter what personal sacrifices she had to make. I love my mother so much. It is hard to hold back the tears when I recollect how hard my mother and father worked to keep our family together. The ten cows, twenty sheep, fifteen pigs, thirty to forty rabbits, and fifty to sixty chickens we raised on our farm are still vivid memories for me. These animals and the farm-land were an important part of our lives and an integral part of our overall survival.

In town, we lived in an old abandoned complex that was once occupied by a beautiful queen (I cannot recall her identity) in the fifteenth century. We shared that complex with eight other families. Our apartment consisted of one large living room, two bedrooms, and a kitchen. With five boys, four girls, and two parents living in such small quarters, there were certainly times when it all felt too small.

One of my fondest memories as a little girl living in Cosenza Rende was listening to my oldest sister,

Rosina, tell us stories during the evening hours. Rosina was simply remarkable with her storytelling skills. "The Three Little Pigs" and "Snow White and the Seven Dwarfs" were among my favorites as a child. I will always remember how cozy and comfortable I felt lying on the living room floor listening to Rosina's voice capture the very essence of each character in her stories.

Since Rosina was the oldest girl, my mother relied upon her considerably to help with the household chores. Washing clothes, cooking, and keeping our house neat and clean were Rosina's daily responsibilities. She worked hard at helping my mother maintain a strong sense of pride and cohesiveness within our family. Even then, I somehow knew that my mother appreciated her efforts and attitude by how much she depended upon Rosina.

Another fond memory of mine was watching my mother teach my brother, Orlando, how to bake bread and make homemade pasta. Orlando was so attentive to my mother's instructions, which was one of the reasons why he became an excellent cook. I also remember my second oldest brother, Ettore, owning his own barber business in our hometown. He developed into a superb barber, and our family benefited immensely from his exceptional skills.

I was enrolled in school for only six months prior to moving to America, but even this short amount of time in school was spent consistently daydreaming about what my life would be like in twenty to thirty years. I wanted so desperately not to live in poverty. The two to three miles that I walked to and from school was spent in thoughts of anticipating what my life would be like in twenty years. In a short period of time, my life was to change forever; I would be on my way to America, and my dreams were about to be fulfilled.

As I stated, my earliest memory is at three years of age saying to myself over and over again, "I will never, never be poor, even if I have to work day and night." I remember praying to God, "I promise I will do anything to succeed — I will help our family. I will help other people in need. Just let me be successful." When I was three years old, I imagined that everything was magic. I would say to myself, "You push a button and everything is gonna go." Little did I know that life does not operate that way.

Before this dream could come true, my mother, my sister Maria, my two brothers, Rocco and Mario, and I had to pass a series of aptitude tests. These tests were administered in Rome by the immigration authorities. If an individual wanted to immigrate to America, then that person would have to successfully pass a reading, verbal, written, and vision test.

Uncle Emilio, my father's brother, deserves special mention at this point; it was he who supervised the entire process of getting all five of us from Cosenza Rende to Rome by way of train in order to take these tests. My dear uncle actually organized five trips to Rome for this purpose, which included trips for my father and his group, my sister Emilia, and Orlando and his family, as well as Ettore and his family. Uncle Emilio supervised the trips for the entire family because he personally knew the people in Rome who handled the immigration process.

Uncle Emilio was a very special individual who worked extremely hard during his life. He was a disciplinarian and a man with vision. Even though he was left physically challenged from a bout with polio in his youth, this never stopped him from making his dreams a reality. At one point in his life, he owned a telephone before anyone else did in his town, and the town's people would come to him to use it. He was the owner of a club where people could come and play cards and he also owned a grocery store and a shoemaker shop.

My uncle was married, and he and his wife raised two sons who later became fine young men. Both of his sons, Pino and Pedro, have been university-educated, which includes both having earned their Ph.D. degrees. Pino has become an outstanding chemist, and Pedro has become a well-respected politician, set to run for a term as senator. My two cousins have in turn raised their families to be respectable and successful Italian citizens.

Uncle Emilio treated us no differently than he treated his own family. He expected us to behave in an orderly fashion and with some sophistication. It was understandable then why he became so incensed with Rocco, who was fifteen years old at the time, when Rocco accidentally broke a bottle of wine while we were dining during our trip to Rome. And it did not make matters any better that Rocco was constantly preoccupied with watching the beautiful women of Rome. My uncle Emilio passed away in 1993, and I dearly miss his presence and influence.

My father, my brother Luigi, and my sister Rosina had already been living here since May 3, 1960 when I moved to America with my mother, Maria, Rocco, and Mario. Emilia moved to America in 1961, and Ettore and Orlando moved to this country with their families in 1968. My father, Luigi, and Rosina were able to immigrate to America through the sponsorship of my Uncle Santo, my father's older brother.

Though it was Uncle Santo whose sponsorship was responsible for my father, Luigi, and Rosina coming to

America, it was Uncle Santo's wife at that time, Rose Tellerino, who sponsored me to come to America. Unfortunately, shortly after my arrival into this country, Uncle Santo and Rose were divorced. Favorably for me, Rose decided to remain connected with our family and she has been a stable force in my life ever since I arrived.

I consider Rose Tellerino to be a great woman. It was Rose who took time out of her life to complete the paperwork that allowed me to come to America. Rose has been an inspiration to me throughout my life because she has lived her life according to the principles of integrity, compassion, and love. She has always been a woman who is devoted to God, her Christian faith, family, and community. Today, Rose is one hundred and two years old, and I feel extremely blessed to have Rose and her positive influence in my life.

My Uncle Santo lived in Chicago, Illinois, and by the time I arrived in America he was on his way back to live in Italy. Uncle Santo was the second male authority figure after my father that I loved, respected, and admired. I remember my uncle as a hard working man, strong, and tall at six feet, two inches. In some ways, he was the opposite of my father, who was five feet, five inches tall, skinny, and if I blew at him real hard, he would fall down.

Don't misunderstand me; my father was also a hard working man, and I loved him very much. My father was actually the first male authority figure that I can remember developing a strong sense of respect and admiration toward. He was a devoted husband to my mother and a devoted father to all of his children. My father always inspired me with words of encouragement whenever I was in the grip of self-doubt or confusion. Though my father may have looked somewhat frail physically when compared to Uncle Santo, he was any-thing but frail on the inside. My father's heart was strong, and he was a courageous and dependable man.

My father was not at all enthusiastic about staying in America or about having the remainder of the family move here. He was forty-nine years old when he moved to America, and even though he wanted to become rich and accumulate material things, he felt very much out of sync with the American way of life. He wanted to become rich in Italy as a farmer. In one year he would have the opportunity to purchase the farmland that he had been tending for fifteen years, so he was very re-sistant to the idea of moving to America.

But my mother wanted out of the farming lifestyle, and she wanted out immediately. I remember how anx-ious my mother would get waiting for the arrival of a letter from my father in America, a letter that usually described his experiences of feeling overwhelmed in a foreign land.

My mother occasionally described to me some of her pre-America conversations with my father. On one occasion, she reported that my father stated, "America: it's for young people." My mother replied, "No, I want my children to have opportunities." To which my father would retort, "No, I want to come back and become rich in Italy." My mother eventually won the battle of words, and we moved to America.

The motivation to move to America was strictly my mother's. She was determined that her children have economic opportunities that were not available to us in our homeland. She wanted her children to have the opportunity to develop careers that would be different than what she had been traditionally groomed to step into, and wearisome farming was out of the question. My mother was absolutely committed to seeing her dream come true for her children despite my father's strong opposition to moving to America.

Some of my mother's siblings had already departed from the old country and moved to either Canada or America. Aunt Saletta would ultimately move to Kamloops, British Columbia, where my mother's older brother, Uncle Luigi, had previously established his new home. Another sister, Aunt Rosaria, and a brother, Uncle George, had settled in Chicago. Uncle George had become a successful businessman who owned his own furniture store. I enjoyed all of my mother's brothers and sisters; they were good and solid people with a strong sense of family.

One of my fondest memories just prior to moving to America is centered around my brother, Luigi. Luigi had arrived in America ahead of us, and he set aside money solely for the purpose of helping the rest of the family move to America. He was fiercely dedicated to the family. I was so proud of my brother, and he soon became a role model for me as well. I remember when I was thirteen or fourteen years old and in the eighth grade, my brother Luigi (known as Louie) bought an apartment building. One of the reasons I admired him so much was because he bought this building to help the family.

There were very few landlords that would rent an apartment to a family with four children. Louie bought the building for investment purposes and to help the family overcome this living crisis. At the same time he purchased the building, he started working at the R. C. Cola Company. He worked extremely hard and helped us considerably: at that time he was a mentor to all of the family, not just me. This was just one of many experiences

I would have growing up in which I observed family members and friends model for me personal sacrifice so that my family as a whole could have a more comfortable life.

When my mother, Mario, Rocco, Maria, and I arrived in America during the early sixties, I remember how on that day there was a blizzard, cold winds, and freezing temperatures. We had never experienced cold weather like that before. I was scared of the unknown, but I was also prepared for any and all challenges. I had prayed and daydreamed for so long about a new way of life that I was not about to allow any opportunity to slip through my fingers that would offer me a life free from hardship and poverty.

Flying from Milan, Italy to New York, changing planes, and then flying to Chicago was both exciting and frightening at the same time. This was the first time I was exposed to so many different people, airplanes, airports, and changing cultures. Everyone walked with a faster pace, talked with unfamiliar accents, and there were so many different kinds of people from different cultures, ethnic backgrounds, and religions. I was terrified and nervous, but up for the adventure. I was preparing to begin a life *made from scratch.*

"I have known Ornella for 32 years and she is not only a good friend, but a great sister-in-law. She has a pleasant personality and is very outgoing. Ornella is always ready to lend support and encouragement."

Helen Ruffolo

CHAPTER 2

BRIDGEPORT:
THE BEGINNING

In the blink of an eye, I had traveled from one part of the world to another. At first, the differences between the Italian culture and the American way of life were overwhelming for me. I had left my old home, where people moved slower, talked with familiarity, and treated one another with a measure of respect, only to arrive in a place where the pace was faster, the language was unfamiliar, and the treatment less than hospitable. However, my anxiety and fear was eased by my dear mother's constant reminder to us that in America the opportunity to experience a better way of life, economically, educationally, and socially, was now available. Her siblings who had already made the move regularly informed her of the advantages to living in America.

I was now nearly seven years old. Everything and everybody seemed so big to me, and to tell the truth, I felt intimidated by the challenges that lay ahead. Having spent so much time back in Cosenza Rende daydreaming about what my life would be like in twenty years seemed unimportant in comparison to what my life would be like here and now in the south side Chicago neighborhood of Bridgeport. Instantly, I had to learn a new language, begin a new school, meet new friends, adopt new customs, and live in a new neighborhood.

Later, as an adult, I would learn that this was far more than what a seven-year-old needed to be faced with at such a vulnerable age. Moving from one residence to another can be a challenging experience for an adult. However, for a young child such as myself to be relocated from one culture to another culture that is located in a far-away country, this can be a traumatic experience. Because of the constant daily challenges during the beginning of my new life in Bridgeport, there were times when I found it difficult to hold onto my mother's words.

Sometimes the possibility felt remote that opportunity was abundant in America and that our way of life would improve dramatically. Difficult challenges faced me everywhere I turned. But this is when I began to experience within myself the courage and determination to persevere. No matter how many difficult days were ahead of me, no matter how scared I was; and no matter how many tears I shed, I was steadfast in my resolution to see it through to the end.

My resolve was immediately tested. My family moved into a four-room apartment on 30th and Wells in Bridgeport, a predominantly Italian-American community. My parents, three sisters (Emilia, Rosina, and Maria), three brothers (Luigi, Rocco, and Mario), and I lived in this tight, cramped space for three months. We then moved into a six-room apartment on 28th and Princeton, still within the Bridgeport community, where we lived for one year.

When I was eight years old, my family moved once more, this time to another six-room apartment on 32nd and Princeton, where we lived for only another year. The landlord asked my parents to move because Rocco and Mario were a little too rambunctious. So, my family and I moved into yet another six-room apartment in the building that my brother Luigi had purchased in 1965. We lived in this apartment on 33rd and Wells from 1965 to 1972. We moved from there to an apartment on 33rd and Wallace when I was sixteen years old, right after the passing of my dear and loving mother.

There is no question that moving five times in nine years created constant distress and a never-ending array of challenges. However, all that I could do during this time was to go with the flow and make the most of what we had as a family. There were certainly times when I disliked having to move. Nevertheless, no sacrifice was too great; we were all on a mission to discover the opportunities existing in America of which my mother so often spoke.

What I remember most about those early years was how difficult it was for my family and I to be accepted into the community. Even though there were many other Italian-Americans living in our neighborhood, my siblings and I were never safe from the taunts and threats of the neighborhood bullies. All neighborhoods have them, and I am certain that we were not specifically singled out for such treatment. However, because we were new to this country, it seemed especially difficult for us.

My brothers in particular had the hardest time. They encountered a lot of pressure from the neighborhood bullies on the way to and from work or school. As a family, we were so involved with establishing a new life for ourselves in Bridgeport and becoming successful, that we often had to stick close together in order to overcome the intimidation. As a result, we perhaps did not make as large an effort to mingle with our neighbors as we could have. Even today, I still feel a heaviness in my heart when I recall how difficult it was for my family to settle into our new life in the face of these challenges.

Not even my youngest brother, Rocco, was immune to the pressure we felt. Because Rocco was small in stature, he was often ridiculed and bullied by a few of the bigger students in the school, which naturally hindered his ability to maintain a consistent focus on his studies. Unfortunately, he often had to defend himself on his own, as there were no other adults outside of the family who could help him. This took an emotional toll on Rocco that made his first years in grade school harsh ones.

It is a problem that is still common today in schools everywhere. Those who are perceived as different are often made fun of and shunned. I have actively worked alongside others who believe as I do that this sort of treatment only does harm to a student and prevents him or her from reaching their full potential.

The Ruffolo family was new to the neighborhood, and as newly arrived immigrants, we had to experience what felt like "a new kid on the block" initiation that never seemed to end. In the beginning, people were standoffish and skeptical of our family. This was just one of the differences between my old homeland and my new home.

In Cosenza Rende, the Italian custom was to welcome a new family into the community with a display of courtesy. But in Bridgeport, the way of life seemed to leave my family seriously wondering if indeed we were welcomed into the community. I do know that some sort of display or gesture to welcome my family and I into the community would have eased the tension that we all felt, including our neighbors. I feel sad and disappointed that these were my first experiences in my new homeland.

Coming home from school, the grocery store, or work was often a harrowing experience because I never knew what to expect from the neighborhood bullies. Intimidation of some sort was a guaranteed daily experience. My siblings and I often had to find alternative routes out of and back into our neighborhood. My mother's words, "In America there is opportunity," were both a dreadful curse and a blessing I anxiously awaited to experience.

This was a blessing because I had a dream that I could look forward to finally becoming a reality. However, on certain days, this felt like a curse because nothing came easy with respect to daily living conditions. With all the difficult challenges I was facing, I found myself very eager to experience the *good times*.

Eventually, my family and I were accepted as part of the Bridgeport community, but it was not without per-severance, determination, and courage on all of our parts; even then, not all of our neighbors accepted the Ruffolo family. A few people on occasion still taunted my siblings and me with verbal abuse. I don't view those individuals as a reflection on the Bridgeport community, however. There is no way to please all of the people all of the time and some people are determined never to accept outsiders or newcomers no matter what.

Since my family was large, we mainly interacted with one another, so there was no need to feel compelled to establish outside relationships. I felt safe and secure within my family, though I would eventually take on a principal role, helping to provide safety, security, and strength for them.

I moved into this position when I was twelve years old when my mother started teaching me how to prepare meals. I continued to experience a great deal of pride in the fact that I soon became extremely proficient in preparing various ravioli dishes. By the age of thirteen, I was regularly assisting my mother with preparing the daily meals. After high school, I assumed the responsibility of cooking for my immediate family, including my uncles, aunts, nieces, and nephews: a responsibility that became permanent when my mother passed away.

Once we moved into Luigi's apartment building, I started babysitting two smaller children whose parents lived in the building. After graduation from grade school, this form of employment became a much bigger enterprise for me. My mother's words, "In America there is opportunity" began to take on a more personal meaning for me at this time.

One regret that I have today as I reflect back on those early years in Bridgeport is that I did not establish more outside relationships. I was so busy helping to take care of my family, studying to complete school, and learning a new language that I did not initially miss my lack of friends. But as I reexamine this period in my life, I realize that maybe some of the difficulty I experienced in being accepted into my community was in part due to the fact that I was not that accessible to my neighbors. However, I could not have done anything different than what I did; my life in my new homeland was all too new, scary, chaotic, and consuming for me to have behaved otherwise.

I am pleased, however, to acknowledge that I did establish important relationships with two caring

Puerto Rican girls that I met in grade school. These girls were friendly, and they welcomed my family and me to the neighborhood with open arms. They were helpful and understanding with regards to the difficulties I was experiencing in learning English and finding my way around the neighborhood. I believe that these two girls were willing to extend themselves to me because they were experiencing the same difficulties as I was.

I often think about where these two women are today and how wonderful it would be to personally thank them for the help they provided me with during this time. So, I will take the opportunity now to say thank you for all your help and support in helping to make my transition into Santa Maria Incorata Grade School a smoother one.

In addition to these two girls, I was also fortunate to establish a relationship with two Italian-American girls that lasted from second through eighth grade. In the beginning of our relationship, they too, were helpful and understanding with regards to the challenges I faced in learning English. As our relationship developed over the years, both sisters were like family to me. When we spent time together, we often listened to one another describe school assignments and experiences. I am truly grateful for their support and friendship throughout our grade school years.

It was also during my experiences in grade school that I began to recognize and nourish my courage, determination, and strength and developed the ability to surpass my own expectations. Later, as I moved into adolescence, these qualities proved to be invaluable as I searched for my vocation. I first attended Santa Maria Incorata where I was placed into the second grade. Three months later, my family moved, and I then attended Santa Lucia Grade School, where I was placed into the third grade.

I cried nearly every day at Santa Lucia because learning the English language was still very difficult for me, yet I knew that whatever it took, I *had* to learn to write and speak the language. I hated the daily spelling bees that Sister Maria had us perform. She would line all the children up, and each child was given a number of words to spell. Sister Maria would say to me, "Spell needle, spell store, spell surprise." As the tears streamed down my face, I realized that I could not spell a single word.

In another incident, Sister Virginia asked me to pronounce the word *horse*. I repeated back to her, *hearse*. Sister Virginia stated, "Do you know what *hearse* means? That's what they carry dead people in." I was so humiliated and embarrassed. One of my male class-mates laughed at me and teased me because I could not properly pronounce the word, so after school I beat him up. Every day I went home from school in tears, and I would cry to my mother, "Ma, I have to learn the language, I have to." She would always reply in her soft and gentle way, "Honey, you will, you will."

So I continued to work hard, and I did learn to write and speak English. In six months, I became the best speller in my class. Sister Maria often addressed my classmate Frankie, a young immigrant boy from Italy, saying, "You see, Frankie, Ornella's been here six months, and she can spell." She would get her paddle and hit Frankie for not spelling a word correctly. This was often a daily routine of the nuns if a student did not perform to their standards.

Today, parents can take legal action against the corporeal treatment of a child, but not during the time I was in school. The threat of corporeal punishment put additional undue pressure on me to learn English. Speaking quite honestly, it is difficult for a child to develop a sense of joy with respect to learning while being exposed to teaching techniques that involve physical and emotional domination.

Nonetheless, my hard work eventually paid off, and I received two double promotions in one year, going from sixth grade to eighth grade. Up until now, I had been two years behind in school, which was another embarrassing issue for me. But by the time I was thirteen years old, I was in the eighth grade where I was supposed to be. I have faced many challenges in my life, but the success that I experienced with learning a new language in a new school system that was positioned alongside a new way of life, I consider one of my greatest triumphs in my life.

I am indebted to two wonderful teachers whom I met while in fifth grade. One was a nun by the name of Sister Patricia, and the other teacher was Ms. Kaufman. Both Ms. Kaufman and Sister Patricia were extremely supportive and helpful to me with my school studies. Even though the English language continued to offer me fierce challenges throughout my grade school years, Ms. Kaufman and Sister Patricia recognized my devotion and dedication to hard work. Overall, I would rate my grade school experiences after the first two years as good because I enjoyed the experience of learning. And I can certainly say that I was up to the task of studying in order to put myself in the position to learn.

In addition, my mother constantly reassured me that I would succeed in school; "just be patient," she always said. My father also affirmed that I would succeed in school by reminding me that I was smart and bright; "just be patient," he said. As I look back on these days, I am so grateful for the encouragement and support of my parents. I am not certain that I could have succeeded without their valuable contributions.

Another valuable contribution to my development was the five summers that I spent in Kenosha, Wisconsin. The main purpose for my visits in the beginning was to babysit my fifteen-month-old niece, Connie, for my sister Emilia and her husband, Mike. My primary duties while they both worked was to take care of Connie, clean house, iron, and prepare their evening meals.

On the weekends, I would go next door to Mike's parents' home and clean house and cook for them as well. Cocetta, Mike's mother, was employed by a local hospital and Mike's father, Settino, was retired. I prepared their meals and kept Cocetta and Settino's home in an orderly fashion. The summers that I spent in Kenosha allowed me to further develop my organization and cooking skills. In addition, my passion for cooking and compassion for other people was greatly enhanced as well, not to mention a discipline and work ethic second to none.

The hardships of being taunted by neighborhood bullies and the unyielding learning challenges in grade school, as well as the summer spent with my sister and her family left me with one significant realization. My father and mother were directly responsible for setting me upon a course in life where I was and always have been committed to supporting and encouraging other family members and friends to meet head-on their daily challenges.

Both of these individuals encouraged me to accept my experiences as stepping-stones to developing inner strength, compassion, and determination. No matter how difficult the task, one must look for the positive and grow from it. I strongly believe that an individual can accomplish his or her dreams as long as determination, courage, and support are in place. I graduated from Santa Lucia a determined, devoted, and courageous young woman because of my parents' devotion to me as their daughter and as a result of experiencing the early roots of my courage and honesty. What was made from scratch was now beginning to take form.

Nella

Nella

**Nella with classmates right after
graduation from Santa Lucia Grade School. The
next challenge after this glorious day was to
begin discovering her talents and skills**

Nella at home helping with family chores

Nella participating in marriage ceremony for next door neighbor during her first year of high school

CHAPTER 3
BREAKING AWAY:
Becoming A Woman

Tutto bene quel che finisce bene! In English: All's well that ends well! When I reached my goal of graduating from grade school, my sense of accomplishment was enormous. I felt excited about my life and the prospect of gaining a foothold in my new environment: an American way of life that promised to help me keep my vow to *never be poor again*.

Now I turned my attention to discovering more about my talents and continuing my education in order to make this vow a reality. Shortly after graduation, my father was able to find employment for me on Chicago's West Side at the Blackstone Manufacturing Company. This company specialized in manufacturing automobile regulators, and my work task was to seal each box just prior to delivery to the various buyers. I worked for this company from June 5 to August 31,1968.

I was both intimidated and thrilled at the prospect of working in a factory. Most fourteen-year-olds don't work in heavy manufacturing factories, but because my father personally knew the owner of the business, I was hired. To my delight, I found myself working alongside my father. This was my first real taste of being employed by someone other than family or neighbors for babysitting. This was also when I experienced for the first time outside of my home a sense of conviction, self-confidence, a good work ethic, and loyalty to my father.

I did not disappoint my father, my employer, or myself. I was always on time to work, never missed a day, and my work performance was consistently critiqued as excellent. Overall, for a fourteen-year-old working at my first place of employment, I would say that I was a very conscientious employee. I enjoyed being a responsible young woman and developing a strong work ethic that reflected my parents' training.

I now come to a significant event in my life that often is too difficult for me to talk about: my mother's illness, which she painfully struggled with for the next four years. During 1968, shortly after I graduated from grade school, my mother suddenly became ill at home, and she was rushed to Mercy Hospital on Chicago's South Side. Doctors performed tests and took x-rays of my mother's stomach, the area in which she gravely complained of pain, but nothing was found that could explain what was causing her such excruciating suffering. After spending a few days in the hospital, she was re-leased to return home.

Though my mother continued to experience a steady decline with respect to her health, her spirit, passion for family, and mental capacity never damp-ened; our lives were to go on as though we had simply hit a bump in the road. Making the most out of adverse conditions was just one of the reasons why I loved her so dearly and passionately. My mother consistently embodied a way of life that exemplified that the glass was always half-full.

I desired to continue my education by attending St. Mary of Perpetual High School, which was within walking distance of my home. I wanted to attend St. Mary's for two reasons: I was told that it was an excellent high school, and most of my grade school classmates had chosen to attend this school. The tuition was more than my parents could afford, so the money that I received from babysitting and the Blackstone Manufacturing Company went towards paying my tuition.

Late that same summer, I also began working as an usherette three evenings a week at the Blackstone Theater in downtown Chicago. What I remember the most about this time in my life was how I always worked — and I mean always. The summer between grade school and high school was one continuous motion of going from my home to the factory and then either to the Blackstone Theater or to babysitting jobs; there was no time for me to enjoy a social life.

I had learned early in life that I could not depend on anyone other than myself to fulfill my needs and desires that pertained to money because my family was financially limited: there simply was no money. If I wanted a good education or job training, then I was the one who had to satisfy these conditions. I also learned that I would have to, on occasion, set aside personal wants and desires in favor of the wants and needs of family members and relatives.

For example, some of the money that I earned during the summer and early fall also went to pay for my sister Maria's tuition at St. Mary of Perpetual High

School. Maria needed help in getting enough money to meet the tuition costs, and my parents could only provide so much. Even though she attended St. Mary's for just one year, I am glad that I could be of help to Maria; I love her dearly.

My relationship with Maria is just as strong today. She often shares with me how she loves and cares about me, and I do the same with her. Family must take care of family; it is a cardinal rule. I learned from my parents, my brother Luigi, and the good nuns at Santa Lucia the importance of giving, so it was no hardship on me to pay for Maria's tuition, only a pleasure.

Around the time that I began attending St. Mary's, cooking became more of a focal point in my life. I began working at Connie's Pizzeria on 26th and Union Avenue after school and on the weekends. Since I had started to develop a passion for cooking, and was by this time planning and cooking for my family and relatives, finding employment where my primary responsibility was cooking was relatively easy. My employment at the Blackstone Manufacturing Company and the Blackstone Theater provided me with experiences that allowed me to feel more confident and self-assured, which made it easier for me when I applied for employment at Connie's Pizzeria.

However, I do recall experiencing periods of frustration with cooking. There were days when it felt like cooking for someone other than myself was taking up too much of my time. During this same period of time, my two older brothers, Ettore and Orlando, and their families had also moved to Chicago from Italy. It became my responsibility to babysit and cook for their children. In addition, I was the one person who was designated by my older siblings to teach my newly arrived nieces and nephews the English language.

On occasions, my mother would hear me complaining about how much of my days and evenings were spent cooking. She would respond, "Learn, learn the cooking. Someday you will be successful and keep the family tradition of cooking alive." So I continued to immerse myself in the experience of learning to cook.

There were other experiences that I wanted to have for myself, such as learning more about the city of Chicago, but there was no time, and my older brother, Luigi, would not hear of it. He would not allow me to go to downtown Chicago except to go to cosmetology school. Luigi always told me that I would "get into trouble." He assumed that because I was a woman I would probably be taken advantage of; he didn't know that his little sister could take care of herself. He was my big brother and very protective of me.

I recall the time when I was sixteen or seventeen years old, and I talked about opening a beauty salon and Luigi absolutely would not agree to the idea. I cried and cried because he always said no in response to my desire to venture out. It didn't matter: Luigi always had the final word and got his way. It may sound as though Luigi was unreasonable and domineering as a brother, but this was not the case.

Luigi was afraid for me because he was worried about how unsafe life could be during this time for a young woman. I know he felt that I could be taken advantage of in certain social situations or business transactions because of the many unethical men he had met since he moved to America. My brother loved me and wanted the best for me, this I am certain of without question. He just did not know how deep my resolve was with regard to not being taken advantage of, even though I was still an inexperienced young woman in many areas.

I attended St. Mary of Perpetual High School for two years. During my freshman and sophomore years at St. Mary's, I often thought of being a lawyer. My interest in civil law and a penchant for helping people were the primary factors that influenced me in this regard. But again, my parents did not have enough money for me to pursue a law degree, nor were we aware of any options regarding financial aid. Even though my years at St. Mary's were difficult and demanding, I continued to feel an excitement about the experience of learning, and I developed a mastery of the English language. The difficulty was in finding the time to complete my homework while taking care of my mother, who had started to experience a dramatic decline in her health while I was in my sophomore year at St. Mary's.

Towards the end of my freshman year at St. Mary's, I began working part-time at Spiegel's retail mail order house so that I could earn more money. This was in addition to babysitting and cooking for my immediate family and relatives and holding down two part-time jobs. During my sophomore year at St. Mary's, I enrolled on a part-time basis into the School of Cosmetology in downtown Chicago because I discovered I had a passion for grooming and styling hair.

The idea of a career in cosmetology really began as a result of cutting, grooming, and styling the hair of my siblings, their children, and relatives. I found that I enjoyed cutting and styling hair. It is often that what initially begins as a means of taking care of one's family soon develops into a means to earn income and express a newly discovered talent. I experienced it both with cooking and with hairstyling.

Needless to say, my life between the ages of fifteen and sixteen was chaotic, demanding, painful, and overwhelming. I was attending high school during the day and the School of Cosmetology in the evenings, working part-time at Spiegel's, cooking and babysitting for my family, and most importantly, taking care of my mother, whose health was rapidly declining. To add to this mix, shortly after enrolling into cosmetology school I began working in Selan's Beauty Salon three hours a day and all day on Saturday as a hair stylist.

My life was like a double-edged sword. One side of the blade was chaotic and maddening, while the other side of the blade was exciting and self-fulfilling as I discovered my talents, strength, and identity. The attempt to balance the scale between taking care of my needs and taking care of my mother and my family's needs had become a major stumbling block with regards to school.

So I decided to drop out of high school in 1971. My mother needed me to take care of her, so I did. My family and I needed money, so I worked. My family and I needed to eat and maintain a household, so I cooked and watched over my nieces and nephews. My high school studies suffered, so I left. However, I did not leave feeling defeated, but rather determined. I promised myself that I would receive my high school diploma, only it would not be in a traditional manner.

I enrolled on a part-time basis into the largest business school in downtown Chicago, Jones Commercial Business School. On the advice of friends who were attending this school and who also thought highly of its curriculum, I began to study for my GED (General Equivalency Diploma), which is the equivalent to having a high school diploma. I also wanted to develop a stronger aptitude for the business world I had entered into regarding cosmetology.

My active participation in cosmetology school was also limited so that I could be with my mother. Family is extremely important in my culture. The personal sacrifices I made to ensure that each member of my family was cared for both physically and economically became a vital part of a way of life that was to teach me perseverance and devotion.

Between 1968 and 1972, my mother consistently experienced severe pain and discomfort in her stomach, but each visit to the hospital revealed nothing. However, on an unsuspecting afternoon in 1972 the pain was well beyond her ability to tolerate it. I was panic-stricken and terrified that she was leaving me. My father, brothers, sisters, and I were frightened. We didn't want Mother to leave us, nor did we want to see her in such pain and agony; this was extremely difficult for us to experience, especially my father. I remember so well how my father's love, devotion, and admiration for my mother was greatly tested during this time.

This time, the visit to the hospital revealed that my mother had a large cancerous tumor in her stomach. An operation was immediately performed to remove the tumor, but unfortunately, this was not enough. For six weeks she lay in her hospital bed fighting for her life while in tormenting pain. I never left her side during those six weeks. My mother was my life, my inspiration, and my love. Then one afternoon, my mother's heart stopped beating. The doctors and nurses were able to revive her only after considerable effort. She was moved immediately to the Intensive Care Unit and within hours developed walking pneumonia.

At the same time that my mother was in the last stages of her life, my father suffered a massive heart attack in the hospital during my mother's final moments as the hospital staff worked furiously to keep her alive. My father was admitted into the hospital immediately, and the medical staff provided him with excellent care. I was extremely relieved to know that he was in good hands, and in time he recovered.

What heightened this entire experience for me to levels of extreme frustration and anxiety was the fact that each time my mother was brought to the hospital, I had to translate into Italian what procedures the doctors and nurses were performing so that my father could understand. I was unable to address my own emotional needs because I was usually standing between my father and the medical staff making certain that everyone understood one another.

With this last trip to the hospital in 1972, I was extremely tired, exhausted, and unable to deal with what was happening to my mother. It would not be until weeks later that I cried and cried about the horrible way in which my mother was leaving this world. It was not until I was finally alone with my thoughts that I could grieve the loss of my beloved mother.

On August 13, 1972, my mother passed away when I was just sixteen years old. I can still recall the feeling of having lost my dearest and best friend. My mother had such a hard life, but she was so strong and persistent. She moved to America for her children, and she worked hard to see that we had the economic and social opportunities that she felt existed in this country.

My mother believed in me so much and always told me that I had the talent and personality to be anything I wanted. I miss her dearly, and I wish that she could have had the opportunity to experience with me some of my personal successes in the restaurant and beautician professions. I also wish she could have had the opportunity to spend time with her granddaughter, Bianca.

After my mother's death, I remember telling myself, "If I can live through the excruciating pain that I have experienced with losing my mother, then I can live through any painful challenge that I come face to face with in my life." I learned as a result of my grief that although I lost a mother, I had gained a stronger and more defined sense of myself. I learned that what does not destroy a person, can make that individual emotionally and spiritually stronger.

With that in mind, I studied for and passed my GED exam while completing my studies at Jones Commercial Business School. I graduated from Jones Commercial Business School in October 1972. I also went back to the School of Cosmetology and completed their curriculum, and in December 1972, received my state license to practice cosmetology. I went to work as a beautician at Josephine Kosi's salon on 30th and Princeton on a full-time basis.

I am indebted to Josephine for giving me the opportunity to work alongside her and the other beauticians. I learned a great deal from this experience that helped me both professionally and personally. Professionally, I learned how to perfect my skills as a beautician, and personally, I learned how to be more mature as a young woman. Thank you, Josephine.

There can be no question as to the feelings of ecstasy and accomplishment that I felt at the end of 1972. It was a year of devastation and a year of revelation. I had begun to piece together my personal recipe for success. I knew now the difference between facing adversity from an intellectual point of view and facing adversity from an emotional point of view. It takes dedication, perseverance, determination, and devotion to weather the storms that cause a person to doubt one's identity and place in this world. A new life made from scratch was now taking shape in the form of a mature and confident young woman: myself.

Nella at eighteen years of age

Jack Curatolo - 10 years old

Jack Curatolo - The Adult

Jack and Nella at work in the early days

Jack beginning his day

Jack

Nella's
Father

Nella

Thanksgiving dinner 1979

A moment of relaxation

Two of the finest chefs at work

Love and partnership at its finest moment

CHAPTER 4
JACK:
The Man

John Cutia's promise to find me a good man started when I was thirteen and lasted until I was seventeen and a half years old. John would consistently say to me, whether visiting with my family in our home or out among the neighborhood, "Nella, I'm going to find you a good man." After listening to his passionate pledge repeated over and over again, which sounded more and more like a matchmaking scheme, I learned to smile and acknowledge John's statement without giving it a second thought.

He would even remark on occasion, "God, you're smart. You have cooked so hard for the family, and you have learned the language fast. Someday I will marry you!" I would simply respond in a teasing tone, "Mr. Cutia, leave me alone." Little did I know at that time that John was indeed quite determined to find me a good man. Quite honestly, I am extremely pleased that his determination paid off with such wonderful results.

John could tease and have fun with all of us; he was a long-time friend of our family. John was a middle-aged, Italian-American, medium-built, robust, and jovial. He had immigrated to the United States from Sicily with his family when he was a little boy. Everyone in the neighborhood seemed to know and like John, and I gathered that this was because he was a genuinely nice man who never said a negative thing about anyone. He knew a lot of people because he was a successful realtor in Bridgeport.

When the remainder of the family, including my-self, had moved into the Bridgeport community in 1968, John befriended our family immediately. It goes without saying that John Cutia was a very important figure in my life. He is responsible for bringing Jack and I to-gether. I am forever indebted to my dear friend, John Cutia, for bringing into my life Jack, a man that I have cherished, loved, and respected from the beginning of our relationship.

By the time I reached my seventeenth birthday I had been working full-time as a beautician at Josephine's Beauty Salon for approximately one year. My babysitting and cooking responsibilities were still a major factor in my life. I considered myself to be an attractive young woman and took pride in my overall appearance; however, boys had no place in my life. There was too much work to be done.

So I was pleasantly surprised and taken aback when John informed me one evening in 1974 that he had met a man earlier in the day who he thought would be an excellent match for me. John had met Jack Curatolo at the Water Market Place, a wholesale outlet for restaurants in downtown Chicago. After he and Jack had spent some time conversing with one another, John said, "I have the perfect woman for you." It seems that the two were discussing how Jack was at a place in his life where he was interested in meeting a nice woman with whom he could establish a long-term relationship.

However, I did not meet Jack right away; it took roughly one year for that to occur. John would often state how he had lost contact with Jack and that he had not seen Jack at the market place. Then, one afternoon John came to our home and mentioned excitedly that he had run into Jack at the market. John said, "This gentleman wants to meet you." My brother Luigi replied sharply and without hesitation, "If he wants to meet my sister, he has to come over to our home. We're not going to him!" John agreed to inform Jack of the arrangements, and the stage was set for Jack and I to meet. I was both nervous and excited at the same time. My older brother had spoken, and my father was in agreement with his handling of the matter.

It was twenty-six degrees Fahrenheit in Chicago on April 12, 1975 when Jack arrived at my home at noon. I could hear the loud engine of the Pontiac TransAm he drove as he pulled up to the house. I can still remember what he looked like on that cold April afternoon. Jack's blue eyes and shoulder-length hair matched his brown leather jacket, brown and white shirt, brown slacks, and boots. I found him quite handsome.

There were seven other family members present to meet him on that day. I had taken special care in preparing the meal that evening. The main dinner consisted of chicken cacciatore, mostaccioli, meatballs, antipasta salad, and an assortment of other side dishes. It was a fantastic dinner, and I was extremely proud of myself for what I had accomplished.

Jack loved the meal, and he complimented me several times on its exquisite preparation and taste. Both during and after dinner, my family members questioned

Jack about where he lived, what he did for a living, how long had he been in America, and who sponsored him to come here. He seemed to handle the pointed questions quite well, and I remember being impressed with Jack's poise and the ease with which he spoke. I eventually came to learn that this was one of Jack's best qualities. Even though Jack was well received by my family, my father remained somewhat cool towards him.

My father did not seem satisfied with Jack's answers regarding being a single man, living alone, and coming to this country with his father. At this time, Jack was twenty-five years old and I was seventeen and a half years of age; my father wanted to make certain that this older man would not take advantage of me. My father and brothers, especially Luigi, were always protective of me. I was both comfortable and uncomfortable with this reality of family life.

On the one hand, it felt natural and loving that my father and brothers wanted to shield me from the evils of this world. On the other hand, it felt restricting and limiting to not experience my strength, authority, and autonomy as a woman capable of asserting myself in response to these evils.

Later on in the evening, Jack and I were able to talk to one another with more privacy and on a more

personal basis. I was pleased to find out that he originally was from a small community in southern Italy that
was only seven miles from my hometown. The more we
discussed our Italy connection, the more we realized
that my family, and especially my father, knew many of
the same people back in our hometown area that Jack
knew. Jack spoke passionately about coming to America
on April 26, 1970 when he was twenty-one years old and
his great anticipation of starting a new life for himself
that would include more economic opportunities.

He mentioned that back in Italy he had been a
construction worker, but now he was the sole proprietor of
his own business. Jack was confident and proud when
he described his hot dog and sandwich shop and how
he got started in the business, which was located on
4219 St. Charles Road in Bellwood, Illinois. Though he
had been in business for himself a mere five months
when we first met, Jack was optimistic and excited about
the prospect of being a successful entrepreneur.

In turn, I shared with Jack my accomplishments,
which included learning to speak and write the English
language quickly, passing my GED, completing Jones
Commercial Business School, working as a full-time
beautician, and having become an outstanding cook,
all at seventeen and a half years old. Jack was pleased
that I had become an independent, yet family oriented

woman; it made for even better conversation that evening. Jack arrived at my home at noon, and he did not leave until ten o'clock that evening. Jack, my family, and I enjoyed the entire day together, and when he left he promised to call me the next day. Although my father enjoyed the festive atmosphere, he was still not completely sold on Gioacchino (Jack in English) Curatolo.

Over the next few days, Jack called me at home, and he occasionally came by the house to visit. We continued to get to know one another better, and I must say I found Jack to be a passionate man who loved to talk and talk and talk. However, a week later Jack telephoned me and in a serious voice confessed to having lied with regards to certain statements that he made the first day he, my family, and I met.

Once my father heard this, he immediately felt validated with some of his concerns regarding Jack. I believe that Jack thought it best to confess because he realized that my family knew some of the same people in our hometown area and that the truth about his past would eventually surface. I also believe that Jack confessed because he was beginning to develop a strong liking for me.

Jack had not told us earlier that he had been previously married for one year in Italy, had one child from this marriage, and his uncle, his father's brother, was the individual who had sponsored him to come to America. His marriage ended in divorce upon returning to Italy after having spent just a few months here in America. Jack was sensitive and compassionate as he painfully described how his ex-wife struggled with distressing personal issues of her own and how this struggle became the basis for a separation and subsequent divorce.

Jack also stated that his mother, who was currently living in Italy, was now raising his daughter. I can still see Jack's face and the conviction in his blue eyes when he shared with me that he had sent several thousands of dollars back to Italy for the care of his daughter, mother, and other family members since returning to America. Jack's strong sense of integrity and commitment were just two of his outstanding qualities that impressed me about him from the beginning of our relationship. Later into our marriage I would learn just how deeply ingrained these qualities were embedded into his character.

He apologized for not telling me the truth about these matters, and he asked me for a second chance, for an opportunity to begin our relationship with complete honesty. He mentioned his fear of rejection as the basis for omitting the truth. What was I to say? How could I be closed off to the idea of forgiveness and a second chance with such a fine display of honesty and account-ability? Plus, Jack did seem like a decent and caring man.

Obviously, I agreed to give him a second chance, even though my father could not as yet warm up to Jack. It would take my father close to nine months to discard his caution and accept Jack with open arms. Nonethe-less, the courtship began, and for the next two and a half months Jack and I would regularly go to the mov-ies, and I continued to prepare great meals for the family, a family that was beginning to include Jack. It was not until two and a half months into our courtship that our lives were changed forever and for the best.

Jack had literally fallen under the spell of my cooking. He loved how I prepared meals, how they tasted, and how each meal was made from scratch. He had an appreciation for the manner in which I cooked meals that seemed to excite his passion to talk. I also believe that Jack had fallen under the spell that I too, was a decent, intelligent, and caring woman. Jack and I enjoyed many wonderful conversations with one another over these dinners. He often shared with me how much he enjoyed my honesty, innocence, strength, and passion.

One evening as we sat and talked about our re-spective days, Jack turned to me and asked if I would come and work for him at his hot dog and sandwich shop. He needed help with getting more visibility for the business and increasing profits. I did not have to consider his offer; my answer was an immediate yes! This new career path represented an opportunity to put my ingenuity, work ethic, and excellent cooking skills to work and finally realize a childhood dream: no more poverty.

Cooking had been in my family for generations, and I always knew that if I were to be successful, I would have to work for myself. I returned to work the following day and informed Josephine that I was leaving her salon to begin a new career in the restaurant business with Jack. Everyone in the salon knew about Jack; after all, we had been a couple for almost three months. Josephine did not want to lose me, especially since I had become the number one beautician in her salon. She tried to persuade me to stay, but I was determined to begin a new career with Jack.

Of course, my father was uneasy with this decision; he still had not warmed up to Jack and he was worried he was losing me. We had some good discussions about my dating Jack and going to work for him, and I could certainly understand my father's genuine concern for my safety. My father wanted to make certain that I would be adequately paid for my services. Both my father and Luigi were hesitant with their approval, but I knew I had their support because I also knew that they wanted me to be happy and to follow my heart. By now I was gaining some credibility with my father and Luigi, I was almost eighteen years old and I had some experience with making good decisions about my life.

One important piece of information that deserves to be mentioned at this point is my relationship with Rosie Cardinale. I first met Rosie when I was ten years old. She and her family, which included her four children, lived in the neighborhood on 30th and Princeton. From the beginning, what impressed me the most about Rosie was her sense of calmness, compassion, and spirituality.

Rosie became a mentor for me after my mother passed away. I would go to her on many occasions and seek her guidance and counsel on matters involving my life, and I always came away from our sessions having learned a little more about myself. I trusted her love for me and valued her wisdom and advice. It was important for me to have a wise and caring older woman in my life that I respected. Rosie was and still is that woman.

One early afternoon, I went to seek Rosie's guidance and counsel with regards to my relationship with Jack. After two months, I thought it wise to share with Rosie my first experience with romance. Rosie was great. She said, "Bring him to my house, I will cook a great dinner for you two, and I will see what he is like." She cooked a fantastic dinner for Jack and I at her home. Afterwards, she informed me that she thought Jack to be a good and considerate man.

At the end of June 1975, I went to work for Jack at his hot dog and sandwich shop, which was called Gioacchino's. In the beginning, Jack would pick me up at home usually around 8:00 A.M. and bring me home at roughly 2:00 A.M. This was our schedule seven days a week, and this lasted for about one year. My primary focus in the beginning was to develop effective marketing strategies to promote the business, and we worked non-stop to accomplish this all-important step towards drawing more customers.

I noticed that Jack was producing great products, but he had no customers. We started advertising heavily in the neighborhood newspapers and utilizing direct mail. I also noticed that Gioacchino's was not listed in the Yellow Pages. Frustrated, I said to Jack one day, "Who is going to call you if you are not listed in the telephone directory?"

I loved the fact that Jack was ambitious, a hard worker, and he knew what he wanted. I also loved the fact that he was a perfectionist, but there would be and still are times that if Jack was in a race with molasses, he would lose the race. I began to realize that he needed someone to match his effort in order to maximize the success of Gioacchino's, and I felt that I was that someone.

Sandwiches were no longer the main items being served at Gioacchino's. We expanded the menu to include pizza, spaghetti, mostaccioli, and roasted chicken. Jack and I did everything by hand because we could not afford to purchase the machinery for processing the pizza dough and sausages. Jack made all the pizza dough by hand - fifty pounds a day, every day, for six months. I was grating cheese with a little grater, not even 12 inches tall - three cases a week. We even made our own sausages - three hundred pounds of sausage a week.

There were many days that we were tired, but we continued to do what needed to be done. Every day, we got up and came to our shop and worked extremely hard to get the food made. We were young, we had a vision, and we both could work non-stop. Business grew like crazy.

Customers stood outside in line to get into our pick-up and delivery restaurant where the food was the best in the area. Jack's perfectionism and my ingenuity made certain that our product was the best. I weighed one hundred and ten pounds when I first started working for Jack. By the time our business started to rapidly grow, I had lost about ten pounds, and my father really began to worry about the soundness of my decision to undertake this new career path.

We worked day and night: just Jack, our four delivery drivers, and myself. The rapid increase in our telephone order business dictated that we hire delivery drivers, since our business was strictly pick-up and delivery. Our little store was only 500 square feet, but we were determined to utilize every inch of space to help ensure our success.

On a Sunday afternoon in June of 1976, Jack and I went to see a movie at a theater on North Avenue. He started talking passionately about how I was the perfect woman for him because we had similar backgrounds and I came from the perfect family. In his next breath, Jack proposed marriage to me. I was breathless and I said, "Yes, yes I will marry you!" I also said to Jack in Italian, "*O. Incotrato luomo del mio sogno.*" Translated this means "I met the man of my dreams."

Rosie's words to me when I once again sought her guidance after Jack proposed marriage were, "Marry him, he worships the very ground that you walk on. He truly loves you." Thank you, Rosie, for being in my life. You are truly a dear and loving person. Your love for Jack and me has been and continues to be an inspiration for both of us.

This was one of the grandest moments of my life. My only regret in that instant was that my mother could not share in my happiness. But I was overjoyed in knowing that I would have my father's blessing. Two months prior to Jack's proposal my father's concerns dissipated, and he accepted my relationship with Jack.

On January 8, 1977, Jack and I were happily married in St. Mary's Church, which is located in Park Ridge, Illinois. Approximately two hundred and fifty friends and family members attended the wedding. The huge reception that followed was also a success. Our honeymoon was spent back in Jack's hometown, Cerisano Cosenza, which was only seven miles from my hometown in the southern portion of Italy.

I still tease Jack today about owing me another honeymoon. I want to spend time with Jack where the scenery is more breathtaking and the two of us can truly enjoy one another with complete relaxation. I felt that we did not have the privacy and the freedom to enjoy one another on our sacred honeymoon, due to a steady involvement with my new in-laws. Suffice it to say that we are working on that second honeymoon as I speak. I love Jack very much.

I can state without exception that no other decision in my life has produced more positive results and greater satisfaction than my decision to marry Jack Curatolo. He is a smart, passionate, devoted, and hard working man. Just as important, he loves and cares deeply for me.

Gioacchino's was closed from January 8 to February 25 while we were on our honeymoon. When Jack and I reopened, our business literally tripled in just a few days. Our loyal customers were glad to return to our restaurant, a place where they would be guaranteed to eat the best food in the Chicago area, *made from scratch*.

Jack and Nella at their bridal shower

**Nella's wedding picture before
going to the church**

**Nella leaving home to go to her
wedding with Jack**

A loving moment shared
by Jack and Nella

Jack and Nella
consummate their
relationship by saying
"I do" to one another

Jack and Nella begin
their new life together

Father kisses
his daughter

Jack, Nella, and
Nella's Father

Jack and Nella arriving at their reception

Coming together

The family joins in the celebration

"Gioacchino's is a family made business. It has a little bit of every member of the family. This is what the success of Gioacchino's has been built upon."

Nella Curatolo

CHAPTER 5
GIOACCHINO'S:
The Restaurant

Even though Jack and I were now happily married and working side by side as a team, the restaurant at 4219 St. Charles Road was still Jack's brainchild; it was his idea and his design. When I came on board, I was working *for* Jack, not *with* Jack. It wasn't until we had established our business as a successful enterprise that I felt that I was a significant part of Gioacchino's.

However, it would take moving our operation out of its 500-square-foot location and into a new 1,200-square-foot location before I truly felt that Gioacchino's was an extension of me. Jack and I remained at 4219

St. Charles Road for seven years. We worked feverishly to create an environment where our customers could enjoy some of the finest entrées in Chicago and receive personalized care that would not be easily forgotten. I believed that Jack and I had the finest pick-up and delivery restaurant in the Chicago area.

Never have Jack and I worked so hard in our lives to transform a dream into reality as we did in the beginning stages of Gioacchino's. The success that we experienced at our first location was the catalyst that enabled me to develop inner conviction and confidence about myself as a woman. I acquired strength and confidence in my ability to create, organize, and produce positive results.

In addition, I experienced the beginnings of my authority, my sense of authorship, and just as important, my self-worth. I truly believed that Jack and I were individuals capable of creating a way of life that was good for people; as a result, we could experience monetary reward for our efforts. We had taken Gioacchino's and given it a personality, an identity, and most of all, a valued reputation.

Jack and I were fortunate to have family members come and work for us, which helped immensely. My sister and brother, Emilia and Mario, my sister-in-law Ida, and my three nephews, Rocco, Sam, and Frankie, immediately come to mind when recalling those individuals who were indispensable during this period of time. Emilia worked for us on a full-time basis. When she was not making her scrumptious salads, she would help with the preparation of food. Mario was our pizza maker and made deliveries to customers.

Frankie worked for Jack and I full-time making pizza and helping out at the counter with customer orders, and his brother, Sam, worked part-time primarily making pizza. My nephew, Rocco, worked during the summers making pizza. Ida helped with the cooking and other functions. I am so appreciative of the quality of work that these individuals committed themselves to, and my heartfelt thanks goes out to all of them for rising to the occasion to help Jack and I begin our business on a positive note.

One afternoon Jack said to me, "Nella, there's a location just two blocks away, and it would be great for us." My response was, "Wonderful! That would be an excellent idea. We can certainly use the additional place to better accommodate our customers and our growth." It had become a physical impossibility to adequately prepare our meals and satisfy our customers at the 4219 address because we were crowded together in a small area. With excitement and anticipation, Jack and I looked forward to moving to another location. So, in 1980 we moved our business eight blocks to 5001 St. Charles Road. It goes without saying that everyone involved, including our customers, enjoyed the new location.

To our astonishment, in a matter of two to three months we had outgrown the 1,200-square-foot location once thought to be our answer to expansion. I attributed our phenomenal growth to our "dinners for two" offered to our customers at the bargain price of $5.95. For example, one dinner for two consisted of eight pieces of chicken, bread, and pasta, which is a lot of food for this price.

The response to this offer was overwhelming, thus making it necessary to hire additional employees in order to handle customer demand. Jack and I had hoped for a favorable response to the marketing idea, but neither of us had envisioned the tremendous response that we received. The immediate question became could we adequately manage such a demand?

The family, once more, was there to help Jack and I respond to the increase in business. My father worked for us on a daily basis. He would cut bread, wrap the dinners, and cut bushels of peppers. It was not unusual for him to cut at least five bushels of peppers a day, which was a great deal of work for a man his age. Mario continued working full-time making great pizza and delivering orders to customers. Mario was simply wonderful to experience as a valuable part of our team.

My nephew Carmine now worked for us on a full-time basis, and he answered telephone orders, counter orders, and performed baking duties. My sister Maria worked for us mainly on the weekends, and she handled counter and take-out orders. My nieces and nephews worked for us on the weekends during the school year and full-time during the summer months. I am truly grateful to all of my brothers, sisters, nieces, and nephews for their help during this time. I also feel proud of the fact that Jack and I were able to pay everyone a decent wage.

Another significant person in the development of Gioacchino's after the move to the 5001 address is Carlo, my nephew. Carlo started working for Jack and I at this new location when he was ten or eleven years old. In the beginning, he worked primarily on weekends, and his duties included slicing cheese, making pizza, and cooking. While attending high school and afterward briefly attending college, he was always committed to working for us and for the success of Gioacchino's.

Carlo distinguished himself as a responsible and conscientious employee, never once hesitating to extend himself beyond his immediate duties. He has since demonstrated an ability to handle a wider range of responsibilities, which is one reason why he is still with us today and working in the capacity as a business partner. I look forward to sharing more about Carlo later in this chapter. But I will say that my life has been greatly impacted by this young man. He reminds me so much of myself when I was his age. His thirst to learn and his work ethic are personality traits that we share in common.

My nephew Carmine deserves special mention as well. He started working for us in 1978 when he was a teenager and he continues to be employed on a part-time basis. Carmine has an engaging personality and a dynamic smile that helps to make our customers comfortable and relaxed as they prepare to experience the fine cuisine at Gioacchino's. He is such a valuable asset to our organization and one day he hopes to manage his own Gioacchino's establishment. I certainly look forward to assisting him in this pursuit should he continue to work toward this goal.

Another measure of our success and recognition came when the two major newspapers in Chicago wrote wonderful articles about the quality of food served at Gioacchino's. As a direct result of such huge public exposure, an immediate increase in customers once more occurred. The first article to appear was in 1980 in the *Chicago Tribune,* and in 1981 the second article appeared in the *Chicago Sun-Times.* The *Tribune* reported that Gioacchino's stuffed, pan, and thick pizzas were voted number one in the western suburbs, and the *Sun-Times* listed our spaghetti sauce, lasagna, and panzarotti as one of the best in the area.

Needless to say our pick-up and delivery service could barely keep up with the increase in customer demand, but somehow we managed. The experience of gaining a wider range of public exposure resulted in increased revenue and increased work as well. This was the time when Jack and I had some of our most intense moments. Jack had developed a new business plan that called for changing Gioacchino's from a pick-up and delivery restaurant to primarily a sit-down restaurant. According to Jack's way of thinking, moving to a new location at 5201 St. Charles Road would provide us with the space to accommodate his new business plan.

I initially took the position that changing from a pick-up and delivery restaurant to a sit-down arrangement would create a host of new problems that we might not be able to overcome. Up to this point, we had been fortunate in our ability to meet the challenges that had presented themselves. I was not certain if we could meet this new challenge. Increased overhead was a major concern for me.

Could the new location handle a sit-down arrangement when it was only two thousand square feet? Where would we find an array of *full-time* employees that would be devoted to the continued growth and success of Gioacchino's? Could we be certain that the customers would be there to support this innovative idea?

All but one of my concerns was adequately addressed. Jack agreed with me on the idea to expand the new location, so we added on another four thousand feet to the already existing two thousand square feet, giving us a total of six thousand square feet. Our staff was mainly comprised of my nieces and nephews, and part-time employees became full-time employees. Jack and I also began to hire people who were outside of the family circle.

My brother Mario and Mike, my brother-in law, were there to work full-time as well. I am indebted to Mario for all his help in making certain that Gioacchino's maintained a high degree of excellence. Mike Salituro worked for us from 1982 to 1992. I am very appreciative of Mike for all the years of service he committed to us and for his outstanding work ethic.

Mike's mother, Cocetta, was always a wonderful mentor for me growing up as a teenager. She was a warm and gentle woman and pleasant to talk with, which was one of the reasons why I enjoyed traveling to Kenosha, Wisconsin during the summers of my youth. With Mike working for us, I could always experience Cocetta's positive influence because he was so like his mother.

Our customers responded to our new business plan by showing up in the multitudes to enjoy their meals in the dining comfort of our new restaurant. The one concern not adequately addressed was the dramatic increase in overheard. Though overhead expense was and continues to be a concern of mine, I began to move away from it as an all-consuming issue because I have learned that this is a part of doing business and is not a problem so long as revenues are good.

From 1982 to 1986 everyone that was involved with the operation of Gioacchino's was working extremely hard to keep pace with the increase in business. Jack and I hired more delivery drivers, which totaled six, and by 1986 we were employing ten delivery drivers. Up to this moment, I thought I knew the meaning of hard work, but it was this time period that gave new meaning to the experience.

My brothers, sisters, nieces, nephews, and in-laws have been such a big help to Jack and I. They have matched our determination to work efficiently and to work together as an organization with relative ease. For instance, my brother Rocco, who had started with us at the 4219 location and is still employed by Gioacchino's, has made pizza, delivered orders to customers, opened up the restaurant for business in the morning, and he has been a co-manager.

My nieces, Dianna and Connie, have worked for us at all three locations, and Michelle and Jennifer have worked at the latter two. All four of my nieces have contributed significantly to the continued success of Gioacchino's. These young women have taken counter and telephone orders, made great sandwiches, and have been quite thorough in keeping our restaurants clean, neat, and orderly.

My nieces, Anna Maria, Nancy, Teresa, Tina, Dedee, and Gina, have worked for Jack and I primarily at the 5201 location, and I am deeply appreciative of their commitment to maintain a high standard of customer service at Gioacchino's. These young women were usually the first contact a customer would have with Gioacchino's, and a significant reason why our customers looked forward to coming back. They would either take customer telephone orders, function as a "bus girl," or waitress.

My in-laws, Helen and Enzo, were also terrific with their contributions. Helen worked at 4219 performing various functions and as a waitress at the 5201 location. Enzo made pizza for us at the 5001 and 5201 locations. I thank both of these individuals for their support and help during the times when it was most needed. Before I move on, I also want to acknowledge Verna L. Pourroy for her fifteen years of employment, inspiration, and devotion to the success of Gioacchino's.

On a personal note, my marriage with Jack was pleasant, loving, and taking on a deeper meaning. We worked well together, both at the restaurant and at home. I developed a deep sense of trust, and I learned that Jack was a dependable individual. He was consistent and responsible for maintaining his part in our relationship. Of course, we had our share of disputes; given the fact that we were also business partners, conflict was ever present. I am a passionate and animated woman, and Jack is conservative and a perfectionist. Even though he and I are different with respect to how we process information, we are thoroughly committed to our marriage and that means working through our disputes.

Mondays were our day off. Jack and I would often go to a movie or find a comfortable restaurant in which to eat dinner. Other times, we visited old friends of Jack's and simply enjoyed one another's company. There were numerous days off that Jack and I would just stay home and keep each other company. Almost from the beginning of our marriage, Jack and I talked of having children. I wanted to have children, but my demanding schedule often interfered with this other dream of mine.

1986 was a year when I felt my best and yet I also experienced the lowest point in my life. This was a year when my heart felt full with joy and it was a year when my heart felt empty and broken. In 1986, Gioacchino's was operating like a well-tuned machine. During the weekdays, we employed an average of fifteen employees, and during the weekends, an average of thirty employees. Business was great, customers were coming in at record numbers, and our profit margin was favorably increasing.

The *Chicago Sun-Times* had written its second article about the fine foods served at Gioacchino's and its continued success. The Italian-American newspaper, *Fra Noi*, which means *Between Us*, had written its first feature article recognizing the accomplishments of Jack and myself. The article was quite complimentary of Gioacchino's, and I am grateful to the staff at *Fra Noi* for their continued support and recognition of Gioacchino's commitment to serving the finest cuisine anyone has ever tasted.

However, the year was not without its tragic moments. During the evening hours of November, one of our delivery drivers was involved in a near-fatal car accident while off-duty and driving his own vehicle. This young man accidentally hit a boy on a skateboard. Because our delivery driver did not have insurance of his own or any personal assets, the parents of the boy filed a lawsuit against Jack and myself for damages. This was made possible because we were not a corporation as yet and because in the backseat of the driver's personal vehicle were empty pizza boxes belonging to Gioacchino's.

All of our drivers make deliveries to our customers in their own cars. Jack and I pay our drivers a daily flat rate for deliveries when they are working. We have never sanctioned nor encouraged our drivers to represent Gioacchino's when they are not working. I was devastated and heartbroken that the court system found Gioacchino's liable for the damages. I continue to feel extremely hurt and disappointed to this day that Jack and I were held responsible for the pain and suffering caused to this young man by a now-former employee while he was neither representing nor working for us.

The amount of restitution we were required by the court system to pay for the damages this young boy suffered was staggering. To add to the misery of this entire experience was the fact that the lawsuit lasted from 1986 to 1990 before it was finally settled.

Though the lawsuit was devastating to me, it was not the most tragic event to occur during this year. In 1968, my father was diagnosed with skin cancer on his nose. The doctors instructed him that he would have to stop smoking immediately if the condition was to be prevented from getting worse. Up to this point, my father was smoking four packs of cigarettes a day. In 1968, when he was told to stop smoking or else, he stopped that very same day. This was the kind of man he was: strong, determined, and not afraid to work to achieve his desired goal.

However, on November 23, 1986, my father fell victim to liver cancer, a disease he was diagnosed with in 1985. A probable cause for the disease no doubt was his years of smoking. My father's death emotionally shattered Jack and I. I still remember how hard Jack cried during the funeral. Both men had become the best of friends over the years. My father was a great inspiration to me throughout my life.

During the last year of my father's life, he continued to work at the restaurant. He would get to work at eight in the morning and leave usually around three in the afternoon. We buried my father in Bridgeport. My only regret with regard to my father's passing is the same regret with respect to my mother's passing. Neither one of them had the opportunity to know their granddaughter, Bianca.

1986 was also the year that Mario was diagnosed with lung cancer. Having already lost my mother to stomach cancer, my brother Orlando to a heart attack in 1979, and now my father, I knew in the back of my mind that it was now time to prepare to lose my dear brother, Mario. Even though Mario maintained a positive attitude toward his treatment, I could observe that he was leaving us. As I mentioned earlier, Mario had worked for us at all three locations, and we had developed a relationship that went beyond the fact that we were siblings.

Mario and I were brother and sister, employee and employer, and most importantly, we were friends. Within two years his cancer had spread so rapidly that it was merely a matter of time before he was to leave us. Mario passed away on August 13, 1988, not quite two years after being diagnosed with cancer. I miss him dearly and I will forever be indebted to him for his love and support of Jack, Gioacchino's, and me.

On a more positive note, from 1986 to 1990, business continued to increase at a steady pace. At one point, customers were lined up outside our restaurant for half a block waiting to get into Gioacchino's. We eventually had to add on another sixty square feet to help accommodate those waiting to dine with us.

In 1990, my sister Maria came to work for us full-time. I am so appreciative of her help with making certain that our customers are properly cared for and for her devotion to the continued success of Gioacchino's. Maria currently is a co-manager and one her outstanding traits is how effortlessly she can engage customers and employees in conversation that can put an individual immediately at ease. I must add that Maria's three sons, Vince, Joey, and Jack, have been valuable employees as well. Vince and Joey work part-time, and Jack works for us on a full-time basis. All three of Maria's sons are exceptional with respect to wanting Gioacchino's to be a continued success.

In 1988, the *Chicago Tribune* wrote its second article commending Gioacchino's fine foods and strongly promoting us as an excellent restaurant to dine at in the western suburbs. In 1990 and 1996, *Fra Noi* wrote two more feature articles promoting the outstanding cuisine served at Gioacchino's, marking Jack and myself as successful entrepreneurs. I feel extremely proud of what Jack and I have accomplished over the years, an accomplishment that would not have been possible were it not for the invaluable help of family and friends.

However, the success of Gioacchino's has not come without great sacrifice and hard work. The constant hard work to make this dream a reality I could and still can accept. The one sacrifice that I could not accept was that I did not have any children of my own. Jack and I both wanted children, but our lifestyle was a major factor intruding on this dream. We decided that it was time to focus and concentrate on making this dream a reality, just as we had made the success of Gioacchino's a reality.

This was in 1992. By 1993, I was frustrated and disappointed that I could not get pregnant. I prayed and prayed to become pregnant, but to no avail. We had purposely left one bedroom untouched throughout the years, hoping to remodel it once I was pregnant with our child. But now, maybe it was time to do something else with that room. Finally, I gave up any hope of becoming pregnant. I felt sad and hurt that I would not experience being a mother. It is funny how in the moment an individual lets go of wanting a dream to become a reality that in the next moment it does.

At first, when I became pregnant, I thought I was experiencing some sort of physical ailment. I had given up any hope of becoming pregnant, so the possibility didn't occur to me. When the doctor announced that I was pregnant, I was flooded with joy and happiness. I was now beginning the journey of being a mother. My daughter, Bianca, was born on June 2, 1994, to two parents that were prepared to give to her the very best that we could: unconditional love, emotional integrity, and a future financially unencumbered.

In 1998, Jack and I sat down together and seriously discussed opening up a second Gioacchino's at a nearby location. For seven years I had been targeting our advertising to the Addison area primarily in response to the ongoing encouragement by our customers who lived here. The comments registered by our customers were for us to specifically open another sit-down restaurant there. However, Jack and I struggled with the question of who would or could run such an operation.

Neither one of us could satisfactorily handle the responsibilities of managing another sit-down restaurant in addition to the 5201 location and raising our daughter, Bianca. It would simply be an impossible task for either Jack or myself. However, we could think in terms of opening another pick-up and delivery restaurant with the right person as its manager. I knew we had just the right individual to manage such an operation.

Carlo was chosen to manage the new Gioacchino's. On May 16, 1998, the new location opened in Addison, Illinois, and Carlo was now officially a business partner with Jack and myself. The second location has been a complete success, and we understand that much of that success is due to the manner in which Carlo manages the business and its customers.

Michelle and Nella

Tina and Nella

Nella and Jennifer

Anna Marie and Nella

Dianna and Nella

Teresa and Joey

Nephew and Nieces

Carlo   Carmine

Carlo at work

**Welcome
to
Gioacchino's**

Ample parking

**Carmine
and
Bianca**

Jack holding Italian zucchini, 5 feet 7 inches long

**Kitchen
Area**

Proud owners of Gioacchino's

Welcome to Gioacchino's

Bianca and Nella

Nella welcomes the customer

Jack   **Nella**

**Nella
and
Jack**

Bianca

Gioacchino's great tasting lasagna

CHAPTER 6
RECIPES:
Made From Scratch

What follows in this chapter are twenty-eight reci-pes that have been primarily responsible for the initial success of Gioacchino's. These recipes are some of our finest, so please join with me in celebrating some of the best meals ever. To achieve the best flavor and taste, use only fresh ingredients.

Linguini in White Clam Sauce

3 (8-ounce) cans of baby clams
¾ cup olive oil, divided
½ cup sherry
2 teaspoons minced garlic
2 teaspoons fresh parsley
¼ teaspoon salt
1 pound cooked linguine
¼ cup olive oil

Sauté garlic in ½ cup of olive oil until tender, but not brown. Add clams, sherry, parsley, and salt, and simmer for 10 minutes. Throw in pasta and toss with ¼ cup of olive oil. Serves 4

Linguini in Red Calamari Sauce

½ cup olive oil
2 teaspoons of garlic, chopped
2 (12-ounce) cans crushed tomatoes
½ cup sherry
2 teaspoons fresh parsley
¼ teaspoon salt
2 pounds calamari, cleaned and cut into rings
1 pound cooked linguine

Sauté garlic in olive oil until tender, not brown. Add tomatoes, and cook for 15 minutes. Add calamari, and cook an additional 15 minutes. Throw in pasta. Serves 4

Linguini with Garlic and Olive Oil

1 cup olive oil
4 tablespoons minced garlic
2 tablespoons fresh parsley
¼ teaspoon salt
¼ teaspoon black pepper
I pound cooked linguine

Sauté garlic in olive oil until tender, not brown. Toss in parsley, salt, black pepper, and pasta. Serves 4

Linguini with Shrimp and Broccoli

¾ cup of olive oil, divided
2 teaspoons of minced garlic
1 pound of fresh broccoli, cut up
½ cup sherry wine
2 teaspoons fresh parsley
¼ teaspoon salt
1 pound of shrimp, cleaned and deveined
1 pound of cooked linguine
¼ cup Romano cheese

Sauté garlic in ½ cup olive oil until tender, not brown. Add broccoli, sherry, parsley, and salt, and cook for 10 minutes. Add shrimp, and cook for another 8 minutes. Throw in pasta, and toss with ¼ cup olive oil and Romano cheese. Serves 4

Mostaccioli in Mushroom Sauce

1/3 cup olive oil
1 medium onion, chopped
2 tablespoons minced garlic
1 pound sliced fresh mushrooms
2 (12-ounce) cans tomato puree
½ cup sherry
1 tablespoon minced basil
1 tablespoon fresh minced parsley
¼ teaspoon salt
1 pound cooked mostaccioli

Sauté onions in olive oil until tender, not brown. Add garlic and do the same. Add mushrooms, tomato puree, sherry, basil, parsley, and salt, and cook for 20 minutes. Toss with pasta and serve. Serves 4

Baccalà

¼ cup olive oil
1 teaspoon garlic sauce
1 onion, chopped or sliced
3 (12-ounce) cans tomato sauce
1 teaspoon dried oregano
1 teaspoon salt
2 pounds codfish
Flour for dredging
Salt and pepper for seasoning
Oil for frying

Sauté onion in olive oil until tender, not brown. Add garlic, and sauté until tender, not brown. Add tomato sauce, salt, and oregano, and cook for 15 minutes. While sauce is cooking, cut codfish into quarters, salt, and pepper lightly on both sides, dip in flour on both sides, and fry in olive oil for 3 minutes on both sides. Put fried baccalà and sauce in a baking pan, bake in a 350 degree oven for 35 minutes. Serves 4

Grilled Calamari

2 pounds calamari, cleaned and cut into rings
1 cup olive oil
1 cup sherry
1 teaspoon minced garlic
2 teaspoons each, fresh parsley and basil
1 teaspoon salt
1 ounce balsamic vinegar for dressing

Marinate calamari in olive oil, sherry, garlic, parsley, basil, and salt for ½ hour. Grill for no more than 15 minutes. Serve with lemon wedges or other condiments. Serves 4

Pasta e Fagiole

¼ cup olive oil
1 tablespoon minced garlic
1 tablespoon fresh chopped parsley
¼ teaspoon black pepper
¼ teaspoon oregano
2 pounds Italian green beans, cut up
½ cup sherry
1 (28-ounce) can plum tomatoes
1 pound ditalini or other small pasta
¼ cup Romano cheese

Sauté garlic in olive oil until tender, but not brown. Add parsley, black pepper, oregano, and green beans, and sauté for 20 minutes. Add sherry and tomatoes, and cook for another 20 minutes. Add pasta, and cook for an additional 12 minutes. Add Romano cheese and serve. Serves 4

Tomato and Onion Salad (Calabrese Style)

8 steak or plum tomatoes, cut into wedges
1 whole onion, chopped
1 tablespoon minced garlic
1 tablespoon each dried parsley, basil, and oregano
1 teaspoon salt
1 cup olive oil

Mix all ingredients together, and serve with a beer or red wine. Serves 4

Marinara Sauce

¼ cup olive oil
½ of a small onion, chopped fine
3 cloves garlic, chopped fine
2 (28-ounce) cans peeled whole tomatoes
2 (28-ounce) cans tomato puree
2 tablespoons fresh basil
1 teaspoon fresh parsley
1 teaspoon oregano
1 teaspoon black pepper
1 tablespoon salt

Heat oil in large pot, and sauté onions until tender, tossing in garlic 1 minute before onions are done. Add tomatoes, and stir in seasonings. Bring to a boil, and let simmer for an hour. Serves 4

Eggplant Parmigiana

14 eggs
½ cup sherry
1 teaspoon salt
1 teaspoon fresh oregano
1 teaspoon fresh sage
1 teaspoon garlic powder
1 teaspoon fresh basil
4 eggplants, peeled and sliced thick
½ lb. flour
1 lb. bread crumbs
½ gallon cooking oil
2 cups Romano cheese
2 cups mozzarella cheese
1 gallon marinara sauce

Mix the eggs, sherry, and seasonings well. Dip each piece of eggplant in the egg mixture, then in the flour, and then in the breadcrumbs, making sure both sides are well coated. Deep fry in cooking oil for 2 minutes on each side. Remove from oil and let cool for 10 minutes. Place a layer of sauce on the bottom of a baking dish, followed by layers of eggplant, sauce, and cheese. Repeat last three layers, and then place in a 350-degree oven, and bake for 30 minutes. Serves 4 to 6

Chicken Gioacchino

½ cup olive oil
½ cup cooking sherry
1 teaspoon salt
1 teaspoon fresh oregano
1 teaspoon chopped garlic
1 teaspoon fresh parsley
1 teaspoon fresh basil
8 pieces chicken
2 potatoes, quartered
2 red sweet peppers, quartered
½ pound fresh mushrooms, whole

Mix the olive oil, sherry, and seasonings well, and marinate the chicken in the mixture overnight. Bake chicken and potatoes in a 350-degree oven for 50 minutes, adding the red peppers and mushrooms 10 minutes before done. Serves 4

Mostaccioli ala Gioacchino

1 pound mostaccioli
2 tablespoons olive oil
1 small yellow onion, chopped fine
2 pounds lean ground beef
1 teaspoon salt
1 teaspoon fresh oregano
1 teaspoon fresh sage
1 teaspoon garlic powder
1 teaspoon fresh basil
2 pounds ricotta cheese
½ gallon marinara sauce

Cook mostaccioli "al dente" and set aside. Heat oil, and then sauté onions until soft. Add ground beef and herbs, and cook through. Let cool for 20 minutes. Mix with cheese, pasta, and marinara sauce, and bake for 20 minutes. Serves 4

Chicken Marsala

1 pound chicken breasts, deboned
Black pepper
Salt
Oregano
Parsley
Flour
2 ounces butter
¼ cup olive oil
¼ cup minced onions
½ cup Marsala wine
½ pound fresh mushrooms, sliced

Combine seasonings to taste, and sprinkle over both sides of chicken. Dip each breast in flour, lightly coating both sides. Heat butter and oil, and then sauté onions until soft. Sauté chicken on both sides until cooked through, about 15 minutes. Add wine and mushrooms, and bake in 350-degree oven for 15 minutes. Serves 4

Easy Vegetable Lasagna

1 lb. mushrooms, sliced
1 large onion, chopped
4 cloves garlic, minced
1 lb. cottage cheese
½ lb. feta cheese, crumbled
½ cup grated Parmesan cheese
1 tsp. fresh oregano
4 cups tomato or spaghetti sauce
1 lb. lasagna noodles
1 pkg. frozen chopped spinach,
defrosted and drained well
4 oz. shredded skim milk mozzarella cheese

Preheat oven to 350 degrees. Combine mushrooms, onions, and garlic in bowl. Cover and microwave for 3 minutes on high. Combine cottage cheese, feta cheese, half the Parmesan cheese, and the oregano. In a microwaveable lasagna pan, layer sauce, noodles, cheese mixture, spinach, and mushroom/onion mixture. Repeat until all these ingredients are gone. Top with mozzarella cheese and the remaining Parmesan cheese. Cover with double plastic wrap. Refrigerate overnight. Remove pan one hour before baking. Microwave on high for 5 minutes. Microwave on medium-high 30 minutes more. Let stand 5 minutes before serving. Serves 8

Garlic Green Beans

Green beans are always plentiful and inexpensive. Here's an excellent way to make ordinary beans sizzle with flavor.

1 lb. green beans, washed and trimmed
and cut into 2-inch pieces
1 small onion, chopped
3 cloves of garlic, minced
2 tbs. butter
1 8.oz can tomato sauce
1 tsp. black pepper
1 tsp. oregano
Salt to taste

Steam beans for 8 minutes until tender and crisp. Sauté onion and garlic in the butter in a small frying pan for 3 minutes. Add tomato sauce and seasonings. Cook 5 minutes more. Add beans, and toss thoroughly to blend flavors and heat throughout. Serves 4

Garlic Peas and Rice

Use aromatic basmati rice for this flavorful dish.
1 tsp. olive oil
2 cups basmati rice
2 cloves of garlic, minced
4 cups water
1 medium onion, chopped
2 cups of fresh peas
1 tsp. curry powder
1 cup diced green pepper

Heat the oil in a large saucepan, and add garlic and onion. Sauté for 5 minutes, and add curry powder, rice, and water. Bring to a boil, and simmer, covered, for 40 minutes or until rice is tender. Add the peas and pepper, and cook 5 minutes more. Serves 4

Pasta Primavera

Any variety of vegetables is great.

½ lb. pasta, such as shells, bows, rotini, or elbow
2 cups New Age Cream Sauce (Also known as ½ and ½ cream in the store)
1 tbs. oil
1 (16-oz) pkg. of frozen mixed Italian vegetables
4 cloves of fresh garlic, cut into slivers
2 tbs. Parmesan cheese

Fill large kettle or 6-quart saucepan with at least 2 quarts water. Add a dash of salt, and bring to a rolling boil. Add pasta, and set timer for 8 minutes. In the meantime, make New Age Cream Sauce and set aside. Sauté vegetables in hot oil for 5 minutes. Drain pasta, and toss with vegetables. Pour New Age Cream Sauce over pasta and toss well. Sprinkle with grated cheese and serve immediately on warm plates. Serves 3

Pasta Salad

A great way to use leftover pasta. Spirals and shells work especially well in this main dish salad that's also a good buffet dish with broiled chicken, roast beef, or fish.

2 cups cooked pasta
2 cups shredded salad greens
1 tomato, chopped
1 cup broccoli flowerets, lightly steamed
¼ cup each black and green olives, sliced
4 oz. shredded Cheddar cheese

Dressing:

¼ cup olive oil
2 tsp. minced garlic
¼ cup wine vinegar
1 tsp. black pepper
¼ cup low-fat yogurt
¼ tsp. dill

Toss pasta with dressing and spices. Let stand to develop flavors. Arrange tomatoes and broccoli on top of salad greens. Top with pasta mixture. Sprinkle with olives and cheese. Serve chilled. Serves 4

Easy Lamb Stew

1-½ pounds of lamb neck bones or shoulder slices
4 medium potatoes, peeled and quartered
4 carrots, peeled and cut into 1-inch pieces
1 medium onion, thinly sliced
2 garlic cloves, crushed
2 teaspoons salt
¼ teaspoon pepper
¼ teaspoon thyme
1 bay leaf
1 cup water

In 3-quart saucepan alternate layers of lamb, potatoes, carrots, and onion. Combine remaining ingredients in small bowl, and pour over ingredients in pan. Cover and begin cooking over medium heat until moisture evaporates. Reduce heat to low, and cook 2 to 2½ hours or until tender. Remove bay leaf before serving. Serves 4 to 6

Mushroom Lamb Chops

4 to 5 lamb or pork chops, ½-inch thick
¼ teaspoon salt
¼ teaspoon pepper
1 (10½-ounce) can of condensed cream of mushroom soup
¼ cup milk

Preheat 10-inch skillet over medium heat for 3 minutes. Add chops and brown on both sides. Season with salt and pepper. Combine soup and milk. Pour over chops. Cover and reduce heat to low when moisture evaporates.

Simmer 20 to 25 minutes or until chops are tender. Turn after 10 minutes. Serves 4 to 5

Glazed Ham

1 (3-lb.) canned ham
12 ounces lemon-lime carbonated beverage

Put ham into 10-inch skillet or 6-quart Dutch oven. Pour carbonated beverage over ham. Cover and cook at medium-low heat for 1 hour. Serves 6 to 8

Honey Glazed Baked Ham

1 (10-12 lb.) fully-cooked ham with the bone
Whole cloves
½ cup honey
½ cup brown sugar
1 teaspoon dry mustard
1 tablespoon orange juice

Preheat oven to 325° F. Place ham, fat side up, on rack in roasting pan. Insert meat thermometer into thickest part of ham, not touching the bone. Bake uncovered for about 2 hours.

With sharp knife remove any skin from ham, and then score ham into 1-inch diamonds. Place a clove in the center of each diamond.

Combine honey, brown sugar, mustard, and orange juice in a 1-quart saucepan. Bring to a boil over medium heat, stirring constantly. Brush half of glaze over ham, and bake 30 minutes. Brush with remaining glaze, and bake 30 minutes or until brown and thermometer registers 140° F. Let stand 10-15 minutes before carving. Serves 18 to 20

Veal Steak with Mushrooms

1--½ pounds veal steak, ¾-inch thick
½ teaspoon salt
¼ teaspoon pepper
1 tablespoon shortening or oil
1 tablespoon flour
1-cup fresh sliced mushrooms or 1 (4-ounce) can of mushroom stems and pieces, drained.
1 tablespoon lemon juice

Sprinkle steak with salt and pepper. Preheat 10-inch skillet. Melt shortening over medium-low heat. Add steak, and brown both sides. Cover, and reduce heat to low when moisture evaporates. Simmer 30 to 35 minutes or until tender. Remove veal to warm serving platter.

Stir flour into meat juices, stirring until thickened and smooth. Increase heat to medium-low, and gradually add 2/3-cup water, stirring constantly until thickened. Add mushrooms and lemon juice. Cook 5 minutes, stirring frequently. Spoon over steak before serving. Serves 4 to 6

Golden Fried Chicken

1 (2-1/2 to 3 lb.) frying chicken cut into serving pieces
½ cup flour
1-½ teaspoons salt
½ teaspoon pepper
1 cup vegetable oil or shortening

Wash and dry chicken pieces. In a paper or plastic bag or shallow pan, combine flour, salt, and pepper. Coat chicken evenly with flour mixture.Preheat 10-inch skillet with oil over medium heat for about 3 minutes. Add chicken, and brown about 5 minutes per side. Remove pieces as browned. Remove all but 3 tablespoons of the oil from skillet. Add chicken, reduce heat to low, and cook covered for 30 minutes. Uncover and cook an additional 15 minutes. Serves 4 to 5

Italian Meatballs and Spaghetti Sauce

Sauce:
½ cup vegetable oil
1 cup chopped onion
1 clove garlic, crushed
1 (2-lb., 3-oz.) can Italian tomatoes, undrained
2 (6-oz.) cans tomato paste
¼ teaspoon fresh oregano leaves
1 teaspoon salt
1/8 teaspoon pepper
1 teaspoon fresh basil leaves
2 tablespoons fresh chopped parsley
½ cup water

Preheat 3-quart saucepan, heat oil over medium heat about 3 minutes. Add onion and garlic. Sauté for 5 minutes. Add tomatoes, tomato paste, oregano, salt, pepper, basil, parsley, and water.

Cover and bring to a boil over medium heat. Reduce heat to low and simmer 1-½ hours, stirring occasionally.

Meatballs:

1 pound lean ground beef
½ pound veal
½ pound ground pork
¼ cup packaged flavored dry breadcrumbs
1 clove garlic, crushed
¼ teaspoon pepper
2 eggs slightly beaten
½ cup milk
1 teaspoon fresh basil leaves
¼ cup fresh chopped parsley

In large mixing bowl combine beef, veal, pork, breadcrumbs, garlic, pepper, eggs, milk, basil, and parsley. Mix well. With moistened hands, shape mixture into meatballs 1-½ inches in diameter.

Preheat 10-inch skillet over medium heat. Add a portion of meatballs to cover bottom of skillet. Brown on all sides. Place into sauce after browning. Continue browning remaining meatballs. Cover and continue simmering sauce and meatballs over low heat 45 to 60 minutes. Serve over hot cooked spaghetti with grated Parmesan cheese. Serves 6 to 8

Nella's Chicken Soup

1 (2½ lb.) chicken
3 cloves of garlic, chopped
2 carrots, sliced
2 stalks of celery, sliced
1 medium onion, chopped
Salt and pepper to taste
2 quarts of water
1 cup of uncooked rice or noodles

The day before serving, combine chicken, garlic, vegetables, water, and seasonings in a large stockpot and
simmer for 2 hours. Do not add rice or noodles. Let
cool and remove chicken and vegetables. Set aside.
Refrigerate broth overnight, covered. In the meantime,
skin and de-bone the chicken. Keep 2 cups of chopped
chicken meat for the soup and use the rest for other
purposes. Save the vegetables in a covered container
and refrigerate. The next day, 30 minutes before serving,
skim the fat off the top of the broth and return the liquid
to a large saucepot. Add the reserved chicken chunks,
vegetables, and rice. Simmer for 30-40 minutes. If using
noodles, add to pot 10-15 minutes before serving.
Serves 8

Pasta with Sausage

3 quarts water
½ lb. sliced sausage (turkey, veal, or pork)
2 tsp. olive oil
½ onion, sliced
1-cup tomato or spaghetti sauce
4 cloves garlic, cut into slivers
1 tsp. black pepper
½ lb. sliced mushrooms
½ lb. pasta
½ cup grated Parmesan cheese

Heat 3 quarts water in large saucepan. In the meantime, place the remaining ingredients (except pasta and
cheese) in a large skillet. Cook over medium heat, stirring
frequently. When the water boils in the saucepan, add
the pasta. Cook uncovered for 10 minutes. Drain in a
colander, and toss with sauce ingredients in the skillet,
mixing well. Top with cheese, and serve on warm dinner
plates. Serves 4

Nella, Jack, and Bianca in their garden

CHAPTER 7
BIANCA:
The Next Generation

I feel particularly blessed by the birth of my daughter, Bianca. I say particularly blessed, because after many disappointing years of trying to become pregnant, my dream of having a child was finally a reality. Once more, I was reminded that if I can maintain my faith and not attempt to control the result, then I am more likely to realize my dream. Although I would have felt the same total ecstasy and jubilation about giving birth to a boy, having a daughter has given a special meaning to my life.

My mother sacrificed a great deal of her life by insisting that our family move to America so that her children could experience better economic, educational, and social opportunities than what existed in Italy at the time. She could have been content to remain in Italy and concentrate primarily on the wishes and needs of herself and my father. But my mother was not satisfied with experiencing mediocrity for herself, my father, or for her children. My mother was a woman with integrity and vision, and part of her vision included a commitment to go to any lengths necessary to elevate the standard of living for her children.

I personally have accepted this same challenge to elevate the standard of living for those individuals whose lives I may touch. I take this challenge seriously, and those who have a history with me will attest to my steadfast approach to this legacy handed to me by my mother. Without question, I am solely committed to elevating and improving the economic, educational, and social opportunities for Bianca.

My mother and father modeled for their children solid examples of going to any lengths to improve a way of life by respecting and giving value to an individual's life. My mother insisted on her children learning more about their individual talents and developing these talents to such a degree that our lifestyles would be enhanced and free from working for another individual. She wanted us to avoid the oppressive lifestyle of farming that she knew both as a child and as a woman. My father went to considerable lengths, possibly sacrificing his dream of becoming rich, in order to support my mother and her dream that her children know another way of life besides farming. Bianca will experience the same commitment from Jack and myself. Assisting Bianca in the development of her individual talents and skills is our utmost commitment.

My pregnancy with Bianca was truly a delightful experience that seemed to bring out the best in me. Except for a skin rash that I developed during the fifth month of pregnancy, my physical health remained in excellent condition. During my pregnancy, I worked out on a treadmill for an hour a day, five days a week. In addition, I continued to work a forty-hour workweek at the restaurant.

My emotional health was excellent as well, which was evidenced by my playfulness. For example, I was more humorous at work and home. Although I certainly had my days when I was moody, these days were the exception and not the norm. I attribute having a good disposition to feeling very blessed that I was pregnant with a child that soon would be a wonderful extension of Jack and myself.

Nine days before I gave birth to Bianca, my sisters, and nieces put together a spectacular baby shower in which one hundred and forty-five women came to share in the occasion. I was overwhelmed with gratitude by the expression of love demonstrated for both Bianca and myself by my sisters, nieces, and friends on that unforgettable evening. We shared fun and laughter like I have never before shared with such a large gathering of women. For hours we exchanged jokes and talked about some of the craziness taking place in our daily lives.

I worked right up to the day before Bianca was born. After working my usual eight hours on Wednesday, June 1, 1994, I went into labor that evening at 9:00 P.M. At first, I did not think anything unusual about the fact that I was experiencing a wet sensation; I was momentarily unaware that my water had broken. Once I recognized that I was beginning labor, my sisters, Maria and Emilia, and my niece, Gina, rushed me to the hospital without delay. All three were in an immediate standby mode, which I deeply appreciated. Come to think of it, all of my family and relatives were in a state of alert with respect to making certain that I got to the hospital once I began labor.

I often tease Jack about how nervous and anxious he was during the later stages of my pregnancy, which was why I did not bother to telephone him at work until I was well into labor. Even when Jack arrived at the hospital, he was far more anxious and nervous about the birthing process than I. Much of my immediate focus was on the painful labor that I was experiencing, so there wasn't time to feel nervous and anxious about the delivery of our child. However, I can vividly remember that I was the one in labor about to give birth to Bianca, and yet I was also the one giving Jack emotional and physical support so that he could figure out what to do next. At one stage during my labor process, it was difficult to determine which one of us was about to give birth.

I was in labor for fourteen hours, and Bianca was born the following Thursday afternoon, June 2, 1994 without complications. My family and friends were in the delivery room alongside the medical staff. It was a great comfort for me to know that my brother Luigi and my nieces, Connie (and her husband, Peter), Michelle, and Jennifer were among the early ones to arrive.

Maria and Emilia were very emotional with respect to me about to give birth, so someone other than myself needed to help bring a sense of calm to event. This whole ordeal became even more amusing, because my dear and sweet husband had to be attended to also. Jack had experienced sympathetic labor pains right along with me.

At birth, Bianca weighed seven pounds and nine ounces and was twenty-one inches long. She was full of life and alert from the very beginning. When the nurse first brought Bianca to me, I instantly felt the incredible bond between mother and daughter. I felt relaxed with her, and I could feel how relaxed she was as she lay in my arms.

Jack, by this time, had some composure, and I could see in his sweet blue eyes just how proud he was to be a father to our newly arrived daughter. I began to breast-feed Bianca immediately and from that very moment to when she first started drinking out of a glass, she never drank from a bottle. I was delighted that she never tired of my natural love and nourishment.

I always thought as a child how important it was to be attentive to what my mother had to say and what she was doing; no one had to teach me this, it just came naturally. From the beginning, it has been the same with Bianca. She is curious, intelligent, and attentive to everything I do and say. One might suggest that I am making this statement because I am her mother, and therefore I am speaking from a biased position. Regardless, I have developed an exceptional ability to accurately judge the personality of people over the years, and I feel that my daughter possesses some remarkable character traits.

I extend a warm and heartfelt thanks to my personal physician, Doctor Patel, for taking good care of me during our twenty-two year association and for referring me to the excellent gynecologist who performed the delivery. The medical team lead by Doctor Schangle and Bobbie, the head nurse, was outstanding in their support, and I extend my deepest gratitude to Elmhurst Hospital for a pleasant stay.

Jack was great as well; he never tired of assisting me with Bianca once she was born. He was consistent with his support and love for me, and Jack was a proud father who never tired of expressing his love and admiration for our newborn daughter. Connie, my niece, was fantastic as well. For example, she put a lot of work and time into preparing the extra bedroom in my home for Bianca. I had a lot of help from family and relatives when Bianca was born and I am extremely grateful for this support and assistance.

My stay at home with Bianca lasted six weeks before I returned to work. The workday usually began at nine in the morning, and I would leave the restaurant at two in the afternoon. As soon as Bianca was born, Jack began remodeling a room at the 5201 address to accommodate me in taking care of her needs. This was another way in which Jack demonstrated his support and love for Bianca and myself.

What necessitated my return to work was that I was needed to help make certain that the flow of business at both locations would continue in an orderly fashion. My absence had created some disruption to the normal flow of internal operations for both locations. For example, making certain that our food supplies for both locations was being properly maintained.

There were many days when I took Bianca with me to the restaurant. At times, my niece, Connie, took care of Bianca at the restaurant when it became necessary for me to step away and perform certain duties. Connie was excellent with Bianca, and the two developed an endearing bond.

From the very beginning, Bianca was exposed to a large network of relatives that loved her unconditionally and made certain that she was cared for both emotionally and physically. Aside from this, I feel very proud that Bianca and I were never separated from one another, even when I may have been thoroughly engrossed in tasks involving our restaurant business. I always could manage to oversee the operation at both locations and take care of my daughter's needs.

When Bianca was about two months old, a friend of the family, Bishop Imesch, baptized her at a beautiful Catholic Church, St. Philip the Apostle, in Addison, Illinois. St. Philip the Apostle is our home parish and where Bianca currently attends preschool. I first met Bishop

Imesch in 1987, and I could not imagine anyone other than this loving and humble man, head of the Joliet Archdiocese, performing Bianca's baptism. The ceremony included a sit-down dinner that was attended by many friends and relatives. The occasion was joyous and reverent, and Bianca was absolutely terrific. When she was being baptized, she never cried or indicated in any way that she was uncomfortable. She seemed to glow throughout the ceremony.

Bobbie from Elmhurst Hospital was also in attendance. Her love and fondness for Bianca has always been a pleasure to experience for both Bianca and myself. In the past, I have not experienced people in the medical profession who were willing to take time out of their personal lives to involve themselves in the lives of their patients. Bianca's baptism was truly a special event that was attended by extraordinary people who all shared a deep appreciation for the consecration of my daughter.

As I stated earlier, I believe that Bianca is an exceptional child. At seven months old, she called out one day, "Moma." This was the first time she spoke. Bianca was walking at nine months old and she was running at eleven months old. I am amazed at my daughter's ability to communicate her thoughts and feelings, as well as to grasp so easily what is taking place around her. In addition, I find it delightful to observe Bianca enjoying being a little girl while in the company of other children, as well as adults. I believe that Bianca is happy and excited about who she is at this stage in her life.

One experience that I wanted Bianca to have was to be in a beauty pageant. When she was seventeen months old, I enrolled her in a beauty pageant for children two years of age, and she won first place. Bianca was awarded first place because of her beauty, charisma, and that she was quite photogenic. This is the only beauty pageant that she has been in, but my objective for enrolling her was accomplished. I wanted Bianca to gain some experience in developing poise, steadiness, and confidence, which she did. This was quite a successful experience for both of us.

I look forward to continuing to support her in the development of her curiosity, creativity, autonomy, and personal authority as she grows into adolescence and young adulthood. Jack and I are already financially committed to investing in Bianca's college education. I would like her to attend medical school and become a doctor. Bianca would be a natural at helping other people. But I know that I cannot force Bianca to accept a profession simply on my say-so; this has to be of her own choosing.

I do know that whatever my daughter chooses as a career, she will be both financially and professionally successful. Bianca has an inherent sense of devotion and determination that I observe daily, plus she possesses the sweetest disposition. I know, I know, these last few words are from a biased mother, but I can't help myself.

There is one last piece of information that I would like to share and that involves the nanny that I hired to help me with the care of Bianca. When Bianca was a year old, I hired a woman by the name of Helen Guy. At first, she was not certain if she wanted the position, due to personal time restraints. However, after resolving for herself personal commitments that would have interfered with the time required to adequately fulfill the position, she accepted. I describe this situation because there stood a chance in the beginning that we may not have had the opportunity to experience Helen and have her in our lives.

I feel so fortunate to have Helen in my life and I am extremely grateful that Bianca has the opportunity to have Helen as her nanny. Helen is kind, loving, considerate, devoted, organized, thorough, and loyal. Bianca absolutely loves and adores Helen, and she refers to Helen as "Grandma." Helen has been in our employ for four years and she is treated as a family member; I would not accept less. When I watch Bianca interacting with other people, I am struck by her confidence and stability. There is no doubt in my mind that this is directly related to the fact that Helen is in her life.

I believe that children who are fortunate enough to have adults in their lives who are committed to the child's emotional and spiritual well-being are children who will exude a genuine respect for self and others as adults. As Bianca begins grade school this fall, I know she will be supported in *who* she is as an individual. Jack and I are very committed to making certain that Bianca always has in her life adults who are more than willing to teach her respect and dignity by being respectable and treating others with dignity. Jack and I want to make certain that Bianca is equipped with a solid *recipe for success*.

**Bianca at two months
with Mom and Dad**

**Bianca at three months
with Mom**

**Bianca and
Dad share an
intimate moment**

**Bianca at six
months with
Mom and Dad**

Bianca testing a few items

Bianca becoming comfortable with walking

Bianca coming down the stairs

Bianca and Aunt Maria

Bianca at eleven
months with Mom

Bianca enjoying a
moment with Dad

Bianca enjoying the
trophies that she won at
the beauty pageant

Bianca enjoying her
Halloween oufit

With Dad on her birthday

Bianca in various poses and with a classmate

The Beginning

Bianca's First Christmas

With Dad under the peach tree

The Present

With Mom in a loving portrait

The Dream Continues

CHAPTER 8
CONCLUSION:
The Dream Continues

Up to this point, I have made no mention of the negative feedback that I received from a few friends and relatives who were convinced that I could not be a successful entrepreneur as a woman. I really have no need to focus on this aspect of my history, except to say that Jack and I did encounter a few individuals who felt that the return on our investment of time and money would be slight. In effect, people used to ridicule Jack and I, saying there was no way we could support a family with a little hot dog stand.

However, I turned this negativity to my advantage and used it to help bolster my commitment to accomplish my goal of becoming a successful entrepreneur. When I first collaborated with Jack to make Gioacchino's a prosperous and reputable restaurant, I was absolute in my thinking, and I was willing to go to any lengths to make our venture a successful one. I learned early in my life that in order to be successful in my professional and personal endeavors, changing negative experiences into positive ones is a significant part of that process.

The sentiment constantly expressed to me was that I was a woman and an immigrant, therefore the American Dream was out of my reach. What I have learned instead is that the American Dream can be experienced by anyone who is willing to be persistent and work hard to overcome obstacles and make this dream a reality. Oftentimes, the obstacles include negative experiences that can lead an individual to believe that the American Dream is out of reach: this simply is not true.

My daily challenges in grade school with regards to learning English and especially in learning how to spell taught me that with hard work and determination, I could experience success as a student. The difficult challenges I faced living in a community that was not quite ready to accept a new immigrant taught me that if I remained steadfast in my persistence not to be intimidated, I could eventually experience success as a member of that community. When I first made the vow as a little girl back in Cosenza Rende to never live in poverty again, I was willing to walk through any experience of fear and intimidation.

I learned from my mother and father, two individuals who dedicated their lives to living from a place of honesty and dignity, that I could be a good and successful woman if I, too, committed to this same way of life. My mother, unfortunately for both of us, passed away before she could fully experience the positive results that her devotion, inspiration, and personal sacrifice made possible for me. She was a wise, compassionate, and strong woman. She was also an excellent cook. She taught me how to prepare every meal as though it were a feast. I dedicate this book to the memory and honor of my mother.

I also learned from other women, Sister Patricia, Rosie Cardinale, and Rose Tellerino, how to live as a woman in my strength. And my strength consists of my passion, creativity, compassion, determination, and devotion to be the very best person that I can to others and to myself. The most important lesson that I have come away with from my association with these women is not to be immobilized by fear, intimidation, and the limited perception that women are insubstantial and fragile. I know that I am anything but these ineffective and distorted representations of a woman.

From these women I learned that it was important to be assertive, creative, and loving. When the most
important woman in my life passed away, my mother, it
was the single most tragic moment in my life, but I found
a strength inside of myself I didn't know I possessed.
My mother, Sister Patricia, Rosie Cardinale, and Rose
Tellerino were also strong in their faith as Christian
women. These women mentored me and modeled for
me what it takes to be a successful woman living in our
society. Today, I can boast of a strong faith in God, the
church, humankind, family, and myself. I am indebted
to these women for their stabilizing and positive influence
in my life.

I am also indebted to Father Dino and Father
Angelo for helping me to develop a strong faith in God
when I attended Santa Lucia Grade School. Father
John, my family's parish Priest at St. Philips during the
early ninties, deserves credit as well for his help in
making my faith in God a stronger one. These three
men of God extended themselves to me in such a way
that I could experience first-hand the modeling of compassion and unconditional love.

The early hardships of my brothers and the personal sacrifices they made in order to establish themselves
in a new country have been nothing short of miraculous.
Their individual stories are much too personal for me to

discuss in this book. I only hope that one day each of them will take the time to write their individual autobiographies and share with readers the depths to which they have traveled to live with dignity and integrity. I have been personally impacted by the history that each of my brothers has amassed. The hurt, anger, and disappointment that I have experienced watching them endure persecution as younger men has made me that much more committed to being a woman that can love others unconditionally.

It saddens me that my brothers, Orlando and Mario, have passed away and are not here today to share in our family's success. I felt it was my duty as a loving sister to assist Mario in any way that I could, and I have only fond thoughts and memories with respect to how I honored our relationship. The same is true with Orlando. When he passed away, there was no question that his oldest son, Frankie, was to live with Jack and I that following summer. I supported Frankie and his brother Carmine financially because this was my way of honoring the integrity and dignity that I was committed to embracing; this was my mother and father's legacy.

My sisters have followed the traditional roles that have been historically established for women in society. All four have been thoroughly committed throughout their adult lives to taking good care of their families, and they are to be admired for such dedication and devotion. They, too, experienced early hardships and have made personal sacrifices in order to establish themselves in a new country. The lives of my sisters have been nothing short of extraordinary. Each one of my sisters is a very talented woman, and it is my hope that I can be of support and assist them in realizing their dreams, as they have supported and assisted Jack and me in realizing our dream.

Gioacchino's is a thriving business today because my *recipe for success* has included a lot of hard work, perseverance, and courage. Jack's *recipe for success* has also included the same qualities and commitment to excellence. Yes, we serve some of the finest cuisine, but serving the finest meals does not always guarantee success. It's the attitude and the mental make-up that I attribute much of my success to with respect to Gioacchino's and to my personal life.

An extremely significant attitude that I began embracing as a child is to give thanks for what I have accomplished and accumulated in my life. This philosophy has become a way of life for me that I am extremely dedicated to fulfilling during my life. I have learned how important it is to give to others a portion of what I have accumulated. Throughout my life, *others* have come to mean church, family, close friends, and community.

When people see or hear what I have done to help others I have been laughed at and ridiculed. All of my life I have given to my family, the church, and the community out of a sense of love, gratitude, and conviction. I sincerely believe that God has blessed me with good health, a loving husband, a beautiful daughter, and prosperity. To take any of this for granted would be the greatest sin that I could commit. I have helped so many people over the years, but not because I expected or wanted anything in return. I never expected to be paid back. The people that I helped had no money; when they were financially stable again, the money was needed to keep themselves and their families in order.

Giving from a place of humility and gratitude is an important ingredient for the success of any individual. I have discovered over the years that strength and perseverance mixed with compassion and integrity can create more opportunities for success than any other approach. I say to those individuals who are interested in making the most out of their lives to never let go of their dreams and aspirations. They enhance the conditions of one's life and the lives of others if one is to live rather than merely to survive.

I also say to those same individuals that one must have emotional strength and choose to be mobilized by negativity and fear instead of being immobilized by it. I had to really believe in my dreams of being a successful woman entrepreneur and be willing to work hard. I have said to myself numerous times that with God, anything good is possible. I truly believe that God helps those that are willing to take responsibility to work toward making their dreams and aspirations a reality.

At Gioacchino's, we make our lasagna from scratch; we make all of our sauces from scratch—marinara sauce, meat sauce, Alfredo sauce. We also make all our own manicotti; we make the dough from scratch. Nobody makes the pizza dough at Gioacchino's except Jack and myself. On an average we will go through sixty gallons of sauce each week. All of our meals are prepared in the same manner that I have chosen to live my life: with authenticity, integrity, love, and passion. There is nothing artificial or distorted about Gioacchino's. Our success is built upon being genuine with our meals and with who we are as an organization.

I have written this book to share with readers how a little girl with the determination and courage to be a successful woman, both economically and emotionally, persevered through poverty, misfortune, and cultural confusion to accomplish this goal. My story is not unique by any stretch of the imagination. However, my story deserves to be told because it represents just how far an individual, especially a woman, can go with respect to accomplishing financial independence and integrity.

I want my daughter, Bianca, to make choices in her life that are appropriate and that will enhance who she is an adolescent and an adult. I want Bianca to have educational, career, and financial opportunities that will inspire and encourage her to live as a woman in her strength. I want Bianca to have a good life, one that is based on integrity, passion, faith, and compassion.

As a mother, I know just how impressionable children are. Therefore, I know that in order for my wants to have a strong possibility of occurring, I must continue to model for Bianca a woman who is not afraid to live what I say I want for her. It is my responsibility to my daughter to model for her this *recipe for success* if she is to have an opportunity to *make from scratch* a woman of compassion, integrity, devotion, and passion.

The Dream Continues

AFTERWORD

The first time I met Nella Curatolo, I have to admit that I was a little bit intimidated. I had just taken over as the editor of *Fra Noi*, the Chicago area Italian-American newspaper, and I was calling on her to find out if she wanted to continue advertising and what changes she might want to make to her ad.

I've never had a more efficient conversation in my life. "Yes, I'll continue," she told me. "Here are the changes; I have to get back to work. Thanks for coming. Make sure to fax me a proof." It was over in two minutes, but I had accomplished more in those two minutes than I typically did in two hours with my other advertisers. I left happy, but my head was spinning.

In the course of the next ten years, I have come to know another side of Nella. Sure, she's a no nonsense businesswoman—she had to be in order to do what she's done—but she will give the shirt off her back to a good friend or a worthy cause. She does not suffer fools gladly, but if you win her trust, she is the best friend you could ever ask for. Beneath that hard-driving exterior beats a heart of pure gold. And as devoted as she is to her business, she is equally devoted to her family, friends, and community.

What drives Nella? Above all else, a fierce commitment to excellence. Take the expansion of her business, for example. Often, when successful restaurateurs expand their operations, their food suffers a drop in quality because they have spread themselves too thin. But not at Gioacchino's. When Nella expanded from one restaurant to two, she worked night and day to make sure that her customers were able to enjoy the same great food that they had come to expect.

Nella is equally passionate about her family, and has found creative ways of integrating her roles as mother and entrepreneur. When her daughter Bianca was first able to toddle, Nella removed the central booth in her Bellwood restaurant and replaced it with a play-pen so that she could take care of her daughter while she was taking care of her customers. And as soon as she could talk, Bianca was trundling from table to table, taking mock orders with a little pad and pencil, much to the delight of the customers. The apple doesn't fall far from the tree!

There are many words that describe Nella Curatolo; generous, driven, kind, tough, skilled, and passionate immediately come to mind. But if you had to pick a single word that captures her spirit, that word would be integrity. Nella is one of those rare individuals who always, always does the right thing. People like that are always an inspiration to those around them. It should come as no surprise, then, that everyone who knows Nella is a better person for it.

Paul Basile
Editor, *Fra Noi*
Chicagoland's Italian-American Voice

LETTERS TO THE EDITOR

The following statements were mailed to this editor throughout the publication of this book. Individuals who have been personally impacted by Nella and Jack Curatolo in their respective relationships wrote these statements. As the editor of this publication, I struggled with how many of these statements to share with the reader, knowing that some of them would feel disappointed if their personal statement was not included in this book. I struggled with the question, "Will this information appear as overkill or redundant?"

I finally reached a decision to publish each statement, not because of the disappointment factor or that the reader would be subjected to overkill or redundant information. Instead my decision to publish each statement was based on the consistency of its content and the sincerity expressed in each of the writings. The degree of candor and genuineness in which each individual expressed his or her self with respect to being impacted by Nella and Jack Curatolo was overwhelming and conclusive. I have a responsibility as Mrs. Curatolo's editor to share with her readers a continuation of her story. Please indulge yourself with how integrity, compassion, honesty, and dedication can impact an entire community.

Lorenzo D. Leonard
Editor and Publisher
Puget Sound Press

"Bravo to a terrific woman whose generosity and sincerity for her family and friends is unmatched. She is proof positive that hard work and a positive attitude can make an individual a big success!"

Jill B. Bartnicki – Friend and owner of Jack and Jill's Children's Boutique

"I have worked for my aunt since I was a young boy, and she has taught me many important lessons in my life. Watching her continuously striving to achieve her dreams professionally, as well as personally, my aunt Nella has been able to reach these goals by keeping that ever-important balance between work and family. She has always remembered the significance of family, and she has assisted many of her relatives in reaching their personal dreams. Aunt Nella has been like a second mother to me, and I will forever be indebted to her for the many positive lessons I have learned from her."

Carmine Ruffolo – Nephew

"To Our Dear Aunt Nella:
Congratulations on your book. We truly feel how great it has been that we have had someone such as you in the family who is intelligent and committed to writing a book. We would like to thank you for being our mentor, Aunt Nella. In addition, we have also experienced you as our second mother. Aunt Nella, you are the most caring and loving person we have known. We do not think that there is anything you wouldn't do to help another person. Aunt Nella, you are an extraordinary individual. Love to you always."

Joey, Vince, and Jack – Nephews

"I have had the pleasure of knowing Ornella for over ten years and rarely met anyone with as much courage and determination. Her success is proof positive that anyone with a desire to work hard and have compassion for those around her can realize the American Dream. This book is a testament to a work ethic that embodies all that is good in our society."

Allan J. Gabriele – Certified Public Accountant

"Working with Nella is great. She is very smart and upbeat. I've learned a lot from Nella, and I am still learning from her. She will always provide an explanation as to why certain procedures need to be followed. I personally appreciate this approach, because I feel like Nella is a friend and a teacher. It is a pleasure to be her employee. I wish nothing but much success and great health to her and to her family. Nella really is a great person."

Tony Cicchino – Cook

"Nella Curatolo is a dynamo. The energetic restaurateur, who along with husband, Jack, owns Gioacchino's in Bellwood and Addison, was talking about her latest endeavor, an autobiography and cookbook she has written titled, *Made From Scratch: A Recipe For Success*. In between snippets of conversation, she answered phone calls and questions from her staff as she prepared for another busy day at the Bellwood location."

"Seated in a comfortable teal and mauve booth, the petite brunette said the book is being published by Puget Sound Press in Seattle. Scheduled to be released in July 1999, a cookbook will follow in January 2000. This hardworking business owner, wife, and mother found the inspiration for the book from her own mother. 'I always wanted to write this book because my mom died at a very early age and this book is for her."

"Cutting the restaurant recipes down to a manageable size for the home kitchen required much experimentation. Is she worried that someone might take the recipes and start their own restaurant? She laughed and said, 'You could give somebody a recipe, exactly the same and it never comes out the same. It's what you do with it. It's a lot of love you put into cooking. It's like anything…you raise a child, it's nothing but perseverance and hard work. And who's going to slave in the kitchen? Nobody wants to do that."

"The location at 5201 St. Charles Road is their third on the busy thoroughfare. They started out with a tiny hot dog stand at 4219 St. Charles Road in Berkeley, moved to a slightly bigger location at 5101 St. Charles Road, and then to their present site. Jack Curatolo saw the burnt out Dunkin' Donuts building and envisioned the present day Gioacchino's. The big red and white sign in the parking lot heralds the pizza and pasta restaurant where everything is made from scratch."

"We make our own homemade lasagna, do all our sauces—marinara, meat sauce, Alfredo sauce. We do all our own manicotti; we make the dough from scratch. Nobody makes the pizza dough here except me and my husband. We go through 60 gallons of sauce per week. Nobody has recipes," she said.

"In many Italian families, cooking skills are traditionally passed down from mother to daughter and that was true at the Ruffolo household. ' My mother was a fantastic cook,' said Curatolo. 'At a very early age, my mother taught me how to cook. My mother was making home-made lasagna, homemade raviolis.' By coaxing the pre-teen into learning the fine art of Italian cooking, the youngster found she loved to cook. 'So, every Sunday, I cooked. Every time there was a christening in the family, I cooked. I had a lot of experience," she said.

"Her mother and father, Teresa and Emilo Ruffolo, had arrived from Cosenza, Calabria, in the early 1960s. Convincing her recalcitrant husband to immigrate to America was difficult for Teresa Ruffolo because he had land and a livelihood in Italy. Eventually, she wore down his reserve, and the family, including nine children, settled in the Bridgeport area of Chicago."

"Once there, little Ornella, who later shortened her name to Nella, was the eighth of nine siblings. Feeling the pressure to succeed, she recalled, 'I had to prove to my dad that this was the right choice so I worked very hard in school. The language was very hard at first.' She attended Catholic grade school and high school, honing the writing skills that would serve her well in the future. But when she was 15, tragedy struck when her mother died of cancer at the age of 59."

"In 1974, through a mutual friend, she met the man who would soon be her husband and business partner, Jack Curatolo, who coincidentally was also from Cosenza. She remembered, 'He had a little place at 4219 St. Charles Road. He had a hot dog stand. He had a few Italian dishes, spaghetti, and mostaccioli. I had just graduated and he asked me, "How would you like to work here?" I looked at it and said there was potential.' Her brown eyes sparkled as she smiled and said, 'When you show a man you can do everything from scratch that goes to his heart."

"The tiny place had been open for only six months and there was very little business. Through the duo's efforts, the business grew. After they married in 1977, they went to Italy for their honeymoon and the new bride worried that the business would not be there when they returned. Happily, her fears were unfounded and business tripled upon their return. 'Everybody missed us,' she said. 'We had a really good product. We really believed in the product."

"At first, only the newlyweds worked at the hot dog stand and they did everything including deliveries. 'All this time, we worked seven days a week, side by side for 14 to 16 hours a day,' she said. Eventually, they brought in members of their large extended family. Through the years, the business flourished, but their efforts to have children were unsuccessful until five years ago when daughter Bianca was born. The preschooler now attends

St. Philip the Apostle School in Addison, which is the Curatolo's' home parish."

"The pioneering restaurateurs have been a fixture on St. Charles Road since 1974 and plan to remain there for years to come. Despite those who discouraged the couple from competing in a business that traditionally has a high failure rate, success has proved the naysayers wrong. Nephew and partner Carlo Ruffolo runs the new Gioacchino's Addison restaurant at 613 W. Lake St., which opened May 16, 1998."

"Curatolo attributes their success to 'hard, hard work and perseverance. We have so many traumatic things in our life. Don't let anything stop you, just go after your dream. People used to ridicule us and say there's no way you can support a family with a little hot dog stand. Don't believe what people tell you. I'm the kind of person, if you tell me something negative, I'll turn it into something positive. For all the hard times that I had, I think you become stronger through all your problems."

"A friend and regular customer of Gioacchino's, Paul Basile, is writing the Afterword to *A Recipe for Success*. For ten years, Basile has been the editor of the *Fra Noi*, Chicagoland's Italian-American newspaper. 'I've know her for 10 years and she is one of the most amazing women I have ever met,' he said. 'She is tough as nails, a no nonsense businesswoman. She's hard-nosed, she is driven. At the same time, she epitomizes a heart of gold. She would give the shirt off her back to a good friend and a worthy cause. She is one of those rare people who always does the right thing. She's generous, kind and passionate, but above all, she has integrity."

"When asked what his favorite dish is at the restaurant, Basile replied, 'I love their broasted chicken. The pizza is great. Their calzones are incredible. Now, I have to get off the phone and order one.'"

"The full-time restaurant manager at Gioacchino's in Bellwood is Maria Galione, who is proud of her sister's book. 'It's always been a dream of hers to do this.' she said. 'I have tremendous respect for her. She's reached her high point. Everything she ever wanted, she fought for and she got it.' The recipe for success isn't easy, but the ingredients include hard work, a good attitude, faith in God, family, and love, plus paying the bills and advertising, according to Curatolo. In addition, she said, 'I believe in good quality, I've got a good product.'"

Donna DeFalco – For the New Catholic Explore Publication

"I have worked for Nella almost 15 years. She has been a wonderful boss. Nella is a very kind and caring person not only to me, but also to my entire family. We wish her only the best."

Kim Rodriguez – Waitress

"Dear Aunt Nella,
Your perseverance, hard work, and love for cooking has undoubtedly contributed to the ongoing success of Gioacchino's restaurant. I wish you continued success in the restaurant business and all other aspects of life. Congratulations on your first published book! I am certain that the recipes included in the book will produce a

variety of delicious dishes. As a matter of fact, those recipes may actually improve my cooking skills, which I am sure Mike will appreciate!"

Michelle Schafer – Niece

"Congratulations Nella on your new book. I have known you for 15 years. Your generosity and integrity are something to be proud of. I wish the best to you and your new book. I know every word comes from your heart and written with love."

Nancy – Employee

"I love my mom and dad very much. Mom cooks the best tortellini and other things, and dad makes the best pizza."

Bianca Curatolo – Daughter of Nella and Jack

"I'm the sister of Nella. I have been working at her side for 22 years. I have seen her achieve her goals, and I'm very proud of her. It's always been a dream of hers to write this book, and now that the time has come, I hope she writes many more. I have tremendous respect for her. She's reached her high point in life. Nella, has been a mother, sister, and friend to me. We've been very close, God bless her, and may she have very good luck on her book. I love you very much Nella."

Maria Galione – Sister

"I have known Ornella since I was a little girl. She is a very strong and loving woman. She takes care of her family and all of us who have worked for her over the years. She makes us feel like we are part of the family. I feel because of her I am a better person, and I'm very thankful she is part of my life."

Teresa Conway

"Among the many lessons I have learned from my Aunt Ornella, the one that stands out the most and has become apparent in her success is, if you set your dreams in motion through hard work, determination, and perseverance, they will inevitably become a reality. The opportunities to live life to our fullest potential are endless. The evidence lies in the well-deserved achievements and success of my Aunt Ornella. Best wishes on the release of your new book!"

Jennifer – Niece

"I am one of the cooks for Gioacchino's restaurant. One of the good things about that is that I have the opportunity and the honor to know Nella Curatolo. This memo speaks for itself. Her food is cooked traditionally and in a homestyle, which is developed over the centuries from the great traditional families of the Italian kitchens. She puts in a great deal of love and energy and that indicates that she really cares about people and loves people. It's really an honor to know Nella Curatolo."

Vicenzo Grande – Chef

"For over twenty-six years I have known Ornella Curatolo and have enjoyed her food. Ornella is a take-charge person who settles for nothing but the best. Her accomplishments are exhibited by the success of her various endeavors, the most successful of which is her restaurant, where you can enjoy one of her many pizza, pasta, seafood and other Italian entrees. Ornella's dishes are a favorite among my many clients who return for Ornella's dishes time and time again. Ornella is humbled by her success and takes great pride in commitment to family as a part of her success."

Mr. Jeffrey Mark – Attorney

"I have worked for Nella for three years. Not only is she a good cook, she is also a caring person…if anyone knows, I do."

Willie Joe Oscar – Employee

"Nella is a very hard working woman, a good mother, and a good wife; both come first with her. She works extremely hard at both the Bellwood and Addison locations. She is a generous person, always giving to different charities, and helping people whenever she can. Nella takes excellent care of Bianca. She is always checking on her to see what she is doing, even though I'm with her (ha). Good luck with your book Nella and congratulations. It's a beautiful book!"

Helen Guy – Nanny

"It is such a pleasure to know Nella. She is one of the most successful businesswomen I know. But more than that, she is a person of vision, passion, love, and discipline. She gives 100% plus in all that she undertakes."

Melanie Sahara – Financial Advisor

"Nella approaches her life and dreams like she does her business and cooking——with zest, gusto, pure determination, and warmth! Her life story is tender, joyful, and heartfelt. I feel blessed to have been a recipient of her friendship, her generous spirit, and her energy. She is a true survivor, encouraging all of us to savor the moments and persist even when things seem unbearably tough. Cooking and living from scratch sometimes can be challenging, but as Nella can show all of us, the end result is a feast and a woman who represents a work of art!"

Brenda M. Rodriguez – Director, Center for School and Community Development (North Central Regional Educational Laboratory (NCREL), also friend and personal trainer

"I'd like to give you my opinion of my boss Nella. She's great….She's there when I need her; she helps in every way. I think that she has accomplished what she set out to do with her life. This book is one of her best, besides being a great wife and mom and a good friend. If I could be part of her family, I'd be proud. Good luck and congratulations on your book."

Chris – Employee

"Nella is a supportive wife and a loving mother. And she is also a role model for anyone who has the desire to achieve something. Jack and Bianca can be proud of her. I have worked for the Gioacchino's over a fifteen-year period. I have seen Nella's pride in every dish that is served. I know firsthand of her generosity and I have seen her honest concern for people. She is living out her beliefs that are grounded in God and in family. Her book is her testimony to that."

Verna L. Pourroy – Employee

"Nella has been a customer and a friend of mine for the last eighteen years. She is a perfectionist at everything that she seeks to undertake. She buys only the best products from us, no matter how much it costs because she prides herself on quality. She is a wonderful mother, a wonderful customer, and a great friend. I wish her much success with her book."

Donna

"In addition to managing a wonderful Italian restaurant, Nella Curatolo is a woman who cares about people. Over the years I have come to know her as a person of integrity and compassion. She brings the Italian flair, not just to her cooking, but to her relationships with other people. She is a wonderful human being!"

**Most Reverend Joseph L. Imesch
Diocese of Joliet
Joliet, Illinois**

"Ornella and her husband, Gioacchino (translated into English is Jack), were my first customers when I started my food company, AA-1 Food Distributors, now a division of Ciccone Food Producer, Inc. twenty years ago. They have been loyal customers to my company, and now we are the best of friends. They are very honest and hard working people. I am very glad and happy for them because they were blessed with a beautiful little girl named Bianca. Good luck, Nella."

Sal and Anna Marie Ciccone

"I have known Nella and her family for many years. Though I am her banker, when I visit her restaurant, I feel like family. I have always known her to be an honest, caring, straightforward businesswoman and the best cook around!!!!! I am so glad to hear that she is finally putting all her 'secrets' into a book. I have been trying to get those recipes for years!!!!! Congrats....you deserve it!!!!"

Janice Schoneman
Senior Assistant Manager
Firstar Bank

"Generosity is the first word that comes to mind when I think of my Aunt Ornella. She has always been a very giving person. I wish her the best of luck on her new book. Love."

Connie – Niece

"I have learned to be a hard worker from my aunt and uncle. They have taught me family recipes and to go out into the world and achieve my best. I think my aunt and uncle are strong individuals and hard workers. I wish them the best and much success."

Carlo – Nephew
Diana – Niece

ADDITIONAL PICTURES

Nella and Jack with Emilia and her husband, Mike

Nella with her sisters
Emilia   Rosina   Maria   Nella

Luigi and Ettore

Nella and Maria

Enzo, Carlo, Jack, Nella, Luigi, Carmine

**Bianca
and
classmate**

Jack and Nella enjoying an intimate moment

Jack and niece Teresa   **Nella and Bianca**

A day in the life of Jack Curatolo

INDEX

179

To order more copies of *Made From Scratch*
or for more information about Puget Sound Press,
contact:

Puget Sound Press
6523 California Ave., SW
PMB 292
Seattle, WA 98136
http://www.pugetsoundpress.com
email: thezo@sprintmail.com